**TEACHER'S PET PUBLICATIONS**

LITPLAN TEACHER PACK
for
I Know Why the Caged Bird Sings

based on the book by
Maya Angelou

Written by
Barbara Linde, MA Ed.

© 1995 Teacher's Pet Publications
All Rights Reserved

This **LitPlan** for Maya Angelou's
I Know Why The Caged Bird Sings
has been brought to you by Teacher's Pet Publications, Inc.

Copyright Teacher's Pet Publications 1995

Only the student materials in this unit plan (such as worksheets, study questions, and tests) may be reproduced multiple times for use in the purchaser's classroom.

For any additional copyright questions,
contact Teacher's Pet Publications.

www.tpet.com

TABLE OF CONTENTS - *I Know Why the Caged Bird Sings*

Introduction	5
Unit Objectives	8
Reading Assignment Sheet	9
Unit Outline	10
Study Questions (Short Answer)	13
Quiz/Study Questions (Multiple Choice)	25
Pre-Reading Vocabulary Worksheets	45
Lesson One (Introductory Lesson)	65
Nonfiction Assignment Sheet	68
Oral Reading Evaluation Form	70
Writing Assignment 1	72
Writing Assignment 2	76
Writing Assignment 3	87
Writing Evaluation Form	73
Vocabulary Review Activities	75
Extra Writing Assignments/Discussion ?s	81
Unit Review Activities	88
Unit Tests	93
Unit Resource Materials	125
Vocabulary Resource Materials	137

A FEW NOTES ABOUT THE AUTHOR
MAYA ANGELOU

ANGELOU, Maya 1928- Maya Angelou, one of the greatest voices of contemporary black literature, was born Marguerite Annie Johnson on April 4, 1928, in St. Louis, Missouri. As a child, she lived in Stamps, Arkansas with her paternal grandmother, in St. Louis, Missouri with her mother and her mother's relatives, and in San Francisco, California with her mother. At the age of sixteen she had her only child, Guy, out of wedlock. She was married briefly to Tosh Angelos, a Greek. The marriage lasted only a few years, and they divorced in 1950. In 1973 she married Paul Du Feu, and they were divorced in 1981.

Prior to becoming an award winning author, Maya Angelou was a singer, dancer, actress, playwright, and editor for an English-language magazine in Egypt. She traveled extensively with theater tour groups, and has lived and worked in Egypt and Ghana.

Her first book, *I Know Why the Caged Bird Sings*, was published in 1970. It is her autobiography from ages three through sixteen. The book was nominated for the National Book Award in 1970, and in 1978 was made into a movie for television. This success was followed by a Pulitzer Prize nomination for her second book, *Just Give Me a Cool Drink of Water 'fore I Diiie*, (poetry collection), 1971. Subsequent works include: *Gather Together in My Name* (autobiography), 1974; *Oh Pray My Wings Are Gonna Fit Me Well* (poetry), 1975; *Singin' and Swingin' and Gettin' Merry Like Christmas* (autobiography), 1976; *And Still I Rise*(poetry), 1978; *The Heart of a Woman* (autobiography), 1981; *Shaker, Why don't You Sing?* (poetry), 1983; *All God's Children Need Traveling Shoes* (autobiography), 1986; *Poems: Maya Angelou*, four books, 1986; *Now Sheba Sings the Song*, 1987. In 1992 Ms. Angelou read her poem "On the Pulse of Morning" at President Clinton's inaugural ceremony.

Ms. Angelou is a member of the American Film Institute, The Directors Guild of America, the American Federation of Television and Radio Artists, and is on the advisory board of the Women's Prison Association. She has received honorary degrees from Smith College, Mills College, and Lawrence University. In 1976 she was named Woman of the Year in Communications by *Ladies' Home Journal*. Ms. Angelou was a writer-in-residence at the University of Kansas in 1970, a distinguished visiting professor at Wake Forest University in 1974, Wichita State University in 1974, and Californian State University at Sacramento, also in 1974.

Maya Angelou continues to write, and now lives in Sonoma, California.

INTRODUCTION - *I Know Why The Caged Bird Sings*

This unit has been designed to develop students' reading, writing, thinking, listening and speaking skills through exercises and activities related to *I Know Why the Caged Bird Sings* by Maya Angelou. It includes nineteen lessons, supported by extra resource materials.

The **introductory lesson** introduces students to *I Know Why the Caged Bird Sings*. Following the introductory activity, students are given an explanation of how the activity relates to the book they are about to read. Following the transition, students are given the materials they will be using during the unit. At the end of the lesson, students begin the pre-reading work for the first reading assignment.

The **reading assignments** are approximately thirty pages each; some are a little shorter while others are a little longer. Students have approximately 15 minutes of pre-reading work to do prior to each reading assignment. This pre-reading work involves reviewing the study questions for the assignment and doing some vocabulary work for 8 to 10 vocabulary words they will encounter in their reading.

The **study guide questions** are fact-based questions; students can find the answers to these questions right in the text. These questions come in two formats: short answer or multiple choice. The best use of these materials is probably to use the short answer version of the questions as study guides for students (since answers will be more complete), and to use the multiple choice version for occasional quizzes. It might be a good idea to make transparencies of your answer keys for the overhead projector.

The **vocabulary work** is intended to enrich students' vocabularies as well as to aid in the students' understanding of the book. Prior to each reading assignment, students will complete a two-part worksheet for approximately 8 to 10 vocabulary words in the upcoming reading assignment. Part I focuses on students' use of general knowledge and contextual clues by giving the sentence in which the word appears in the text. Students are then to write down what they think the words mean based on the words' usage. Part II gives students dictionary definitions of the words and has them match the words to the correct definitions based on the words' contextual usage. Students should then have an understanding of the words when they meet them in the text.

After each reading assignment, students will go back and formulate answers for the study guide questions. Discussion of these questions serves as a **review** of the most important events and ideas presented in the reading assignments.

After students complete extra discussion questions, there is a **vocabulary review** lesson which pulls together all of the separate vocabulary lists for the reading assignments and gives students a review of all of the words they have studied.

Following the reading of the book, two lessons are devoted to the **extra discussion questions/writing assignments**. These questions focus on interpretation, critical analysis and personal response, employing a variety of thinking skills and adding to the students' understanding of the novel. These questions are done as a **group activity**. Using the information they have acquired so far through individual work and class discussions, students get together to further examine the text and to brainstorm ideas relating to the themes of the novel.

The group activity is followed by a **reports and discussion** session in which the groups share their ideas about the book with the entire class; thus, the entire class gets exposed to many different ideas regarding the themes and events of the book.

There are three **writing assignments** in this unit, each with the purpose of informing, persuading, or having students express personal opinions. The first assignment is to write a brief autobiography. This will give the students an opportunity to reflect on an event or events in their lives and comment on how the event has influenced them. The second and third writing assignments relate to Maya Angelou's seeking and winning the job on the San Francisco cable cars. The second writing assignment is to develop a resume. This gives students the opportunity to share information about themselves with others, and to develop a skill that can be applied in real life. In the third writing assignment, students will be asked to prepare for a job interview by composing answers to questions they think would be asked in an interview. As Ms. Angelou was the first Negro to be hired to work on the San Francisco cable cars, the students will also be put in the position of being the first of their gender or ethnic background to be applying for a particular job. The purpose in developing the answers to the interview questions is to convince the employer that the student is the best person for the job.

In addition, there is a **nonfiction reading assignment**. Students are required to read a piece of nonfiction related in some way to *I Know Why the Caged Bird Sings*. After reading their nonfiction pieces, students will fill out a worksheet on which they answer questions regarding facts, interpretation, criticism, and personal opinions. During one class period, students make **oral presentations** about the nonfiction pieces they have read. This not only exposes all students to a wealth of information, it also gives students the opportunity to practice **public speaking**.

The **review lesson** pulls together all of the aspects of the unit. The teacher is given four or five choices of activities or games to use which all serve the same basic function of reviewing all of the information presented in the unit.

The **unit test** comes in two formats: all multiple choice-matching-true/false or with a mixture of matching, short answer, and composition. As a convenience, two different tests for each format have been included.

There are additional **support materials** included with this unit. The **resource sections** include suggestions for an in-class library, crossword and word search puzzles related to the novel, and extra vocabulary worksheets. There is a list of **bulletin board ideas** which gives the teacher suggestions for bulletin boards to go along with this unit. In addition, there is a list of **extra class activities** the teacher could choose from to enhance the unit or as a substitution for an exercise the teacher might feel is inappropriate for his/her class. **Answer keys** are located directly after the **reproducible student materials** throughout the unit. The student materials may be reproduced for use in the teacher's classroom without infringement of copyrights. No other portion of this unit may be reproduced without the written consent of Teacher's Pet Publications, Inc.

UNIT OBJECTIVES - *I Know Why the Caged Bird Sings*

1. Through reading *I Know Why the Caged Bird Sings,* students will analyze characters and their situations to better understand the themes of the autobiography.

2. Students will demonstrate their understanding of the text on four levels: factual, interpretive, critical, and personal.

3. Students will practice reading aloud and silently to improve their skills in each area.

4. Students will enrich their vocabularies and improve their understanding of the autobiography through the vocabulary lessons prepared for use in conjunction with it.

5. Students will answer questions to demonstrate their knowledge and understanding of the main events and characters in *I Know Why the Caged Bird Sings.*

6. Students will practice writing through a variety of writing assignments.

7. The writing assignments in this are geared to several purposes:
    a. To check the students' reading comprehension
    b. To make students think about the ideas presented by the novel
    c. To make students put those ideas into perspective
    d. To encourage critical and logical thinking
    e. To provide the opportunity to practice good grammar and improve students' use of the English language.

8. Students will read aloud, report, and participate in large and small group discussions to improve their public speaking and personal interaction skills.

READING ASSIGNMENT SHEET - *I Know Why the Caged Bird Sings*

Date Assigned	Chapters	Completion Date (Prior to Class on This Date)
	Chapters 1-6	
	Chapters 7-12	
	Chapters 13-17	
	Chapters 18-21	
	Chapters 22-24	
	Chapters 25-29	
	Chapters 30-33	
	Chapters 34-36	

UNIT OUTLINE - *I Know Why the Caged Bird Sings*

1 Introduction Non-fiction Assignment PV 1-6	2 Read 1-6 Orally	3 Study ?? 1-6 PVR 7-12	4 Quiz 7-12 PVR 13-17	5 Writing Assignment #1
6 Study ?? 13-17 PVR 18-21	7 Study ?? 18-21 PVR 22-24	8 Study ?? 22-24 Writing Assignment #2	9 Writing Conferences	10 PVR 25-29 Study ?? 25-29
11 PVR 30-33 Study ?? 30-33	12 PVR 34-36 Study ?? 34-36	13 Extra Discussion??	14 Vocabulary Review	15 Writing Assignment #3
16 Movie & Discussion	17 Non-Fiction Presentations	18 Review	19 Test	

Key: P = Preview Study Questions   V = Vocabulary Work   R = Read

STUDY GUIDE QUESTIONS

SHORT ANSWER STUDY QUESTIONS - *I Know Why The Caged Bird Sings*

Note to the teacher: The narrator is referred to as "Marguerite" in the questions that deal with her memoirs, since that is how she refers to herself throughout the book. In instances where the author is sharing her beliefs and philosophy, she is referred to as Maya Angelou.

Chapters 1-6
1. In what style is the book written?
2. What happened to Marguerite at Church?
3. What was Marguerite's dream of what she would one day look like?
4. With whom did Marguerite and Bailey live at the beginning of the book? Why?
5. How does the author say she felt in later years about the stereotyped picture of gay song-singing cotton-pickers, and why?
6. What happened that caused Uncle Willie to "lay low" one night?
7. Describe Marguerite's relationship with Bailey.
8. Describe the living conditions for the whites and Blacks in Stamps.
9. Describe the experience Momma had with the "powhitetrash" children when Marguerite was ten years old.
10. Describe the second incident with Sister Monroe, and its effect on Marguerite and Bailey.

Chapters 7-12
1. Describe the incident in which Momma was referred to as "Mrs." and its effect on the Black community.
2. What, according to the author, was the one thing about the whites that was most enviable?
3. What was Marguerite's concept of God?
4. What reaction did the Christmas gifts from her parents cause in Marguerite?
5. What happened to Marguerite and Bailey when she was seven?
6. Describe the Baxter family.
7. How did Marguerite get the name "Maya?"
8. How did Mr. Freeman treat Marguerite?

Chapters 13-17
1. What happened to Mr. Freeman?
2. What happened to Marguerite as a result of the rape and Mr. Freeman's murder?
3. What happened to Bailey and Marguerite after the doctor said she was healed?
4. Describe Mrs. Bertha Flowers' influence on Marguerite.
5. Why did Momma beat Marguerite and Bailey?
6. How did Marguerite feel about Mrs. Cullinan's shortening her name to Mary?
7. How did Marguerite get out of working for Mrs. Cullinan?
8. Why had Bailey stayed out so late when he went to the movies?

Chapters 18-21
1. What is the author's theory about peoples' belief in divine intervention?
2. What "revolutionary action" took place at the revival?
3. What was the effect of the Black fighter, Joe Louis' victory over his white opponent?
4. How did Marguerite become friends with Louise Kendricks?
5. Why was the friendship with Louise so important to Marguerite?
6. Describe Bailey's relationship with Joyce.

Chapters 22-24
1. How did Marguerite feel about the ghost stories that the customers told in the Store?
2. How did Mrs. Taylor's funeral affect Marguerite?
3. How did Momma interpret Mr. Taylor's vision/dream of his dead wife?
4. Why did Marguerite receive presents from Momma, Bailey, Louise, and others?
5. What happened at graduation that gave Marguerite a presentiment of worse things to come?
6. Describe the graduation speaker.
7. What was Marguerite's reaction to the graduation speech?
8. What happened to get Marguerite back into a better mood?
9. How did the white dentist treat Momma's request to have him take care of Marguerite's toothache?
10. What retribution did Momma demand of Dr. Lincoln for his treatment of her and Marguerite?

Chapters 25-29
1. What did Maya Angelou think was the real reason Momma took her and Bailey to live in California with their parents?
2. What was the enigma of which Maya Angelou spoke?
3. What was the secret world given to Marguerite by Mrs. Flowers?
4. How did Bailey and Marguerite feel about their mother's nervousness on the drive from Los Angeles to San Francisco?
5. How did Bailey and Marguerite learn there were other people in the world?
6. Describe Vivian Baxter's personality.
7. What two events happened at this time in Marguerite's life?
8. What happened to the population of San Francisco's Fillmore district during the early months of World War II?
9. How does the author describe Miss Kirwin, her teacher at George Washington High School?
10. Who, according to the author, is the hero in the Black American ghetto?

Chapters 30-33

1. Where did Marguerite spend her summer vacation?
2. Describe Marguerite's relationship with Dolores.
3. What insight did Marguerite have into her father's personality on their trip to Mexico?
4. What happened to her father while they were at the Mexican bar?
5. How did Marguerite and Daddy Bailey get home from the Mexican town?
6. What was Marguerite's father's reaction when he found out she had a car accident?
7. How did the fight between Marguerite and Dolores start?
8. What did Marguerite do when she left her father's friends' house?
9. Describe Bailey's and Mother's relationship at this point.
10. How did Mother and Bailey resolve their feud?

Chapters 34-36

1. What job did Marguerite want to get, and was she successful?
2. How does Maya Angelou describe the change in her when the spring classes began?
3. According to the author, what forces assault the young Black female?
4. According to the author, why does the adult American Negro female emerge as such a formidable character?
5. What new problem did Marguerite face as a result of reading *The Well of Loneliness*?
6. How did Mother respond to Marguerite's questions about her body?
7. What was Marguerite's solution to her still-present concern over her sexual preferences?
8. What happened to Marguerite as a result of her seduction of the good-looking young man?
9. How did her parents react to her news?
10. Explain Vivian Baxter's statement: "See, you don't have to think about doing the right thing. If you're for the right thing, then you do it without thinking."

ANSWER KEY: SHORT ANSWER STUDY QUESTIONS - *Caged Bird*

Chapters 1-6

1. In what style is the book written?
    It is an autobiography, written in the first person.

2. What happened to Marguerite at church?
    She forgot the words to the poem she was reciting. She became nervous and embarrassed. She left the church to use the bathroom, but tripped on the way out. Once on the porch, her bladder emptied, and she ran home in tears.

3. What was Marguerite's dream of what she would one day look like?
    She thought that one day she would be a white girl with long blonde hair and blue eyes.

4. With whom did Marguerite and Bailey live at the beginning of the book? Why?
    They lived with their paternal grandmother in Stamps, Arkansas. Their parents were getting a divorce and sent the children away.

5. How does the author say she felt in later years about the stereotyped picture of gay song-singing cotton-pickers, and why?
    She was full of rage, because she had seen them coming back, discouraged, with cut fingers an stiff muscles.

6. What happened that caused Uncle Willie to "lay low" one night?
    A black man had allegedly "messed with" a white lady. The Klan was out seeking revenge on the black men.

7. Describe Marguerite's relationship with Bailey.
    He was the greatest person in her world. She describes him as her "Kingdom Come."

8. Describe the living conditions for the whites and Blacks in Stamps.
    The two communities were completely segregated. The whites had refrigerators, but most of the Blacks didn't. The segregation was so complete that most of the Black children had never seen a white person.

9. Describe the experience Momma had with the "powhitetrash" children when Marguerite was ten years old.
    Momma was sitting on the porch when the children came to the store. They mimicked and mocked Momma. Then one of the girls who was wearing a dress but no underclothes did a handstand and exposed herself to Momma.

10. Describe the second incident with Sister Monroe, and its effect on Marguerite and Bailey.
    Sister Monroe approached Reverend Thomas, but he left the altar on the opposite side. Sister Monroe caught up with him and hit him in the head with her purse. His false teeth fell out, and Marguerite and Bailey began laughing hysterically. Uncle Willie took them out of church and whipped them.

Chapters 7-12
1. Describe the incident in which Momma was referred to as "Mrs." and its effect on the Black community.
    A Black man was in court on charges of assaulting a white woman. He told the judge that he had hidden in Mrs. Henderson's store. The judge subpoenaed Mrs. Henderson, and was very surprised to find out that she was Black, since Black women were not addressed so formally. The members of the Black community thought it proved Momma's worth and dignity.

2. What, according to the author, was the one thing about the whites that was most enviable?
    It was their wealth that allowed them to waste.

3. What was Marguerite's concept of God?
    She thought he was white, but not prejudiced.

4. What reaction did the Christmas gifts from her parents cause in Marguerite?
    The gifts made her cry and wonder why her parents had sent their children away. She was convinced that she had done something very wrong to cause it.

5. What happened to Marguerite and Bailey when she was seven?
    Their father came to Stamps and drove them to St. Louis to live with their mother.

6. Describe the Baxter family.
    Grandmother Baxter was almost white in appearance. She was a precinct captain and had considerable leverage in the city. Grandfather Baxter lived for his wife, his children, and his dog. Their six children had reputations of meanness. They were often violent. They were very loyal to one another.

7. How did Marguerite get the name "Maya?"
    Bailey, who was about a year older, used to call her "Mya Sister." This was shortened to "My," then lengthened to "Maya."

8. How did Mr. Freeman treat Marguerite?
   He sexually abused her, and eventually raped her. He threatened to kill her if she screamed, and to kill Bailey if she told anyone.

Chapters 13-17

1. What happened to Mr. Freeman?
   He was arrested for rape, and sentenced to one year and one day in jail. His lawyer got him released the day of the trial. Later that day his body was found, apparently kicked to death.

2. What happened to Marguerite as a result of the rape and Mr. Freeman's murder?
   She stopped talking to everyone except Bailey. She thought that if she talked to anyone, that person might die, too.

3. What happened to Bailey and Marguerite after the doctor said she was healed?
   They were sent back to Stamps to live with Momma.

4. Describe Mrs. Bertha Flowers' influence on Marguerite.
   Mrs. Flowers was the aristocrat of Black Stamps. She took an interest in Marguerite. She told Marguerite that language was the one thing that separated man from the animals. Mrs. Flowers gave her books and told her to read them aloud, and to memorize a poem. Mrs. Flowers gave Marguerite several "lessons in living." Marguerite felt that Mrs. Flowers liked and respected her.

5. Why did Momma beat Marguerite and Bailey?
   Momma overheard Marguerite using the phrase "by the way" when talking to Bailey. She felt the phrase was blasphemous. Jesus was the "Way, the Truth, and the Light," so saying "by the way" was like saying "by Jesus" and this was taking the Lord's name in vain.

6. How did Marguerite feel about Mrs. Cullinan shortening her name to Mary?
   She didn't like it at all. She said every Black person she knew had a fear of being "called out of his name" because of the centuries of insults the Negroes had endured.

7. How did Marguerite get out of working for Mrs. Cullinan?
   Bailey suggested that she drop some of Mrs. Cullinan's favorite china pieces. Marguerite did this, and Mrs. Cullinan fired her immediately.

8. Why had Bailey stayed out so late when he went to the movies?
   One of the actresses resembled his mother. He stayed and watched the movie twice, and was late coming home.

Chapters 18-21

1. What is the author's theory about peoples' belief in divine intervention?
   Poor people attribute their existence and future to divine intervention. As people become more affluent, God descends in responsibility for their lives.

2. What "revolutionary action" took place at the revival?
   The preacher asked all of the ministers to cooperate in referring the newly saved sinners to the church of their choice.

3. What was the effect of the Black fighter, Joe Louis' victory over his white opponent
   The Blacks listening in the store in Stamps were delighted that a Black man had proved that they were the strongest people in the world. They were also cautious about going home in the dark, for fear that some angry whites would take the white fighter's defeat out on them.

4. How did Marguerite become friends with Louise Kendricks?
   They met in a grove of trees while attending the summer picnic. They held hands and watched the sky.

5. Why was the friendship with Louise so important to Marguerite?
   Louise was her first childhood friend. From Louise, Marguerite learned what girls giggled about.

6. Describe Bailey's relationship with Joyce.
   Bailey had his first sexual experience with her. He stole candy from the store to please her. After a few months, she ran off with a railroad porter. Bailey became uncommunicative after she left. He and Marguerite had one brief conversation about her, and then never mentioned her again.

Chapters 22-24

1. How did Marguerite feel about the ghost stories that the customers told in the Store?
   She hated and dreaded them.

2. How did Mrs. Taylor's funeral affect Marguerite?
   It was the first time that the burial ceremony had meaning for her. She finally realized the grim reality of death.

3. How did Momma interpret Mr. Taylor's vision/dream of his dead wife?
   She told him it probably meant that his wife wanted him to work with the children and teach a Sunday School class. She also encouraged him to take in a local boy to help with the farm work.

4. Why did Marguerite receive presents from Momma, Bailey, Louise, and others?
   She was graduating at the top of her eighth grade class.

5. What happened at graduation that gave Marguerite a presentiment of worse things to come?
   The students were ready to sing the Black National Anthem, as they had rehearsed, but the choir director and principal told them to sit down instead.

6. Describe the graduation speaker.
   He was Mr. Edward Donleavy, a white man from Texarkana.

7. What was Marguerite's reaction to the graduation speech?
   It made her angry and sick at heart. He was assuming that the Black students would become athletes, farmers, maids, or have other lowly jobs, while the white students would go on to college and whatever professions they chose.

8. What happened to get Marguerite back into a better mood?
   After the white men left, Henry Reed, the class valedictorian, turned to his classmates and led them in singing the Black National Anthem. Marguerite realized that she was proud to be a member of the Negro race.

9. How did the white dentist treat Momma's request to have him take care of Marguerite's toothache?
   He told Momma to take her to the Negro dentist in Texarkana. He said that he "would rather stick my hand in a dog's mouth than in a nigger's."

10. What retribution did Momma demand of Dr. Lincoln for his treatment of her and Marguerite?
    Momma had lent him money, interest free, during the Depression. She now demanded that he pay her interest on the money. The ten dollars she asked for covered the price of the visit to the Negro dentist.

Chapters 25-29

1. What did Maya Angelou think was the real reason Momma took her and Bailey to live in California with their parents?
    She thought it was because of the incident when Bailey saw a dead colored man, and helped take his body into calaboose for the white sheriff.

2. What was the enigma of which Maya Angelou spoke?
    It was the "humorless puzzle of inequality and hate."

3. What was the secret world given to Marguerite by Mrs. Flowers?
    It was books.

4. How did Bailey and Marguerite feel about their mother's nervousness on the drive from Los Angeles to San Francisco?
    The nervousness made her seem more human to them. They were also glad they had the power to upset her.

5. How did Bailey and Marguerite learn there were other people in the world?
    They learned it through food. Their mother took them to many ethnic restaurants.

6. Describe Vivian Baxter's personality.
    She was jolly at times, but merciless. She was passionate, quick-tempered, and melodramatic.

7. What two events happened at this time in Marguerite's life?
    The United States declared war on Japan, and her mother married Mr. Clidell.

8. What happened to the population of San Francisco's Fillmore district during the early months of World War II?
    It became less Asian and more Negro.

9. How does the author describe Miss Kirwin, her teacher at George Washington High School?
    Miss Kirwin was in love with information. She treated the students respectfully. She was stimulating instead of intimidating. Miss Kirwin never seemed to notice that Maya Angelou was Black and different (there were only three Black students in the school.)
    On later visits to the school, Maya Angelou wondered if Miss Kirwin knew she was the only teacher she remembered.

10. Who, according to the author, is the hero in the Black American ghetto?
"... the hero is that man who is offered only the crumbs from his country's table but by ingenuity and courage is able to take for himself a Lucullan feast."

<u>Chapters 30-33</u>
1. Where did Marguerite spend her summer vacation?
    She spent it in Southern California with Daddy Bailey.

2. Describe Marguerite's relationship with Dolores.
    They didn't like each other. Marguerite thought Dolores was mean, petty, and pretentious. Dolores thought Marguerite was tall, arrogant, and not clean enough.

3. What insight did Marguerite have into her father's personality on their trip to Mexico?
    She realized that he must have been frustrated living in Stamps. He had aspirations of grandeur. She also discovered that under his facade, he was lonely and constantly searching for his place in the world.

4. What happened to her father while they were at the Mexican bar?
    He got drunk, went off with a Mexican woman, and was eventually brought back to his car.

5. How did Marguerite and Daddy Bailey get home from the Mexican town?
    She drove them as far as the border (even though she didn't know how to drive.) By then, he had sobered up enough to drive them the rest of the way home.

6. What was Marguerite's father's reaction when he found out she had a car accident?
    He talked privately with the border guard and the driver of the other car. They all emerged laughing. Later he commented that he didn't know she could drive, and asked if she liked his car. That was all he ever said about the accident.

7. How did the fight between Marguerite and Dolores start?
    Marguerite overheard an argument between Dolores and her father, in which Dolores accused him of letting his children come between them. He left the house. Marguerite tried to assure Dolores that she had no intentions of coming between them, but Dolores accused her of eavesdropping. Then Dolores called Vivian Baxter a whore. Marguerite slapped her and Dolores cut Marguerite.

8. What did Marguerite do when she left her father's friends' house?
    She spent the next month living in an abandoned car in a junkyard with a group of homeless children she met.

9. Describe Bailey's and Mother's relationship at this point.
    They were arguing. He was trying to gain her acceptance by acting and dressing like the men she liked. She didn't realize this, and didn't want him to see him exploited. In a fit of anger, she ordered him out of the house, and he complied.

10. How did Mother and Bailey resolve their feud?
    They talked at his new apartment and agreed that he needed to be out on his own. She arranged with a friend to get him a position with the Southern Pacific Railroad.

<u>Chapters 34-36</u>

1. What job did Marguerite want to get, and was she successful?
    She wanted to work on the San Francisco street cars. It took a while, but she was successful, and became the first Negro to work on the San Francisco streetcars.

2. How does Maya Angelou describe the change in her when the spring classes began?
    "Without willing it, I had gone from being ignorant of being ignorant to being aware of being aware. And the worst part of my awareness was that I didn't know what I was aware of."

3. According to the author, what forces assault the young Black female?
    The young /black female is assaulted by the common forces of nature, masculine prejudice, white illogical hate and Black lack of power.

4. According to the author, why does the adult American Negro female emerge as such a formidable character?
    It is "an inevitable outcome of the struggle won by survivors."

5. What new problem did Marguerite face as a result of reading *The Well of Loneliness?*
    She thought she was a lesbian.

6. How did Mother respond to Marguerite's questions about her body?
    She smoked cigarettes, drank a beer, and showed Marguerite a picture of the female anatomy that was in the dictionary.

7. What was Marguerite's solution to her still-present concern over her sexual preferences?
    She decided she needed a boyfriend.

8. What happened to Marguerite as a result of her seduction of the good-looking young man?
    She became pregnant.

9. How did her parents react to her news?
   They were very supportive. They bought her maternity clothes, took her to the doctor, and told her not to marry the boy if she didn't want to.

10. Explain Vivian Baxter's statement: "See, you don't have to think about doing the right thing. If you're for the right thing, then you do it without thinking."
    Mother was encouraging her that she did know how to take care of the baby.

MULTIPLE CHOICE STUDY/QUIZ QUESTIONS - *Caged Bird*

<u>Chapters 1-6</u>

1. In what style is the book written?
    A. It is fiction, written in the third person.
    B. It is non-fiction written in the third person.
    C. It is an autobiography, written in the first person.
    D. It is a biography written in dialog with the first and third person.

2. Which of the following did **not** happened to Marguerite at church?
    A. She threw up.
    B. She forgot the words to the poem she was reciting.
    C. She became nervous and embarrassed.
    D. On the porch of the church her bladder emptied, and she ran home in tears.

3. True or False: Marguerite dreamed that one day she would look just like her mother.
    A. True
    B. False

4. With whom did Marguerite and Bailey live at the beginning of the book,?
    A. They lived with an aunt in Los Angeles.
    B. They lived with their older sister in St. Louis.
    C. They lived in a foster home in San Francisco.
    D. They lived with their father's mother in Stamps, Arkansas.

5. True or False: In later years the author says she was full of rage about the stereotyped picture of gay song-singing cotton-pickers, because she had seen them coming back from the fields discouraged, with cut fingers an stiff muscles.
    A. True
    B. False

6. What happened that caused Uncle Willie to "lay low" one night?
   A. He had accidentally given a white customer the wrong change. He was afraid the man would come back and steal all of their money in retaliation.
   B. He had been flirting with another Black man's girlfriend. The man was drunk and jealous, and was looking for Willie.
   C. A black man had allegedly "messed with" a white lady. The Klan was out seeking revenge on the black men.
   D. Uncle Willie had been missing church. the church Elder was on his way over to talk to him, and Uncle Willie didn't want to see him.

7. Describe Marguerite's relationship with Bailey.
   A. She was jealous and they fought all of the time.
   B. He was the greatest person in her world, her "Kingdom Come."
   C. He teased her and insulted her, but she still cared for him.
   D. They mostly ignored each other because they didn't have any common interests.

8. Describe the living conditions for the whites and Blacks in Stamps.
   A. The wealthy of both races lived together in the rich section of town.
   B. The town was completely integrated.
   C. Stamps was a completely Black town.
   D. The two communities were completely segregated.

9. With whom did Momma have the following experience when Marguerite was ten years old? Momma was sitting on the porch when they came to the store. They mimicked and mocked Momma. Then one of them who was not wearing underclothes did a handstand and exposed herself to Momma.
   A. It was the Black girls from a rival town.
   B. It was the "powhitetrash" children.
   C. It was a few of the town woman who were drunk.
   D. It was the rich white girls who did it on a dare from their sorority sisters.

10. Which of the following did **not** happen during the second incident with Sister Monroe?
    A. Sister Monroe tackled Reverend Thomas and wrestled him to the ground.
    B. Sister Monroe hit Reverend Thomas in the head with her purse.
    C. Marguerite and Bailey began laughing hysterically when the Reverend's false teeth fell out.
    D. Uncle Willie took them out of church and whipped them.

Caged Bird Multiple Choice Questions Chapters 7-12

1. What effect did the incident in which Momma was referred to as "Mrs. " have on the Black community?
    A. They thought it proved Momma's worth and dignity.
    B. They thought it proved she was richer than the white people.
    C. They thought it proved how holy and reverent she was.
    D. They thought it showed that she was too good for them, and should leave town.

2. What, according to the author, was the one thing about the whites that was most enviable?
    A. It was their white skin.
    B. It was their self-confidence.
    C. It was their wealth that allowed them to waste.
    D. It was the fact that they could go anywhere they pleased.

3. What was Marguerite's concept of God?
    A. She thought each race had their own God.
    B. She thought God was white, but not prejudiced.
    C. She thought God was female, and preferred Black females over others.
    D. She did not believe in God, but kept her own beliefs secret for fear of punishment.

4. True or False: The Christmas gifts from her parents made Marguerite cry and wonder why her parents had sent their children away. She was convinced that she had done something very wrong to cause it.
    A. True
    B. False

5. What happened to Marguerite and Bailey when she was seven?
    A. She skipped a grade and entered Bailey's class.
    B. Momma got remarried.
    C. They saw their first white person close up.
    D. Their father came to Stamps and drove them to St. Louis to live with their mother.

6. Which of the following does not describe the Baxter family?
    A. Grandmother Baxter was almost white in appearance.
    B. Grandfather Baxter lived for his wife, his children, and his dog.
    C. There were eight children, four boys and four girls.
    D. The children had a reputation for being mean and violent.

7. True or False : Marguerite got the name "Maya" because when she was little she used to take Bailey's toys and other things and say "mya." The adults thought it was cute and started calling her "Maya."
    A. True
    B. False

8. How did Mr. Freeman keep Marguerite from telling on him?
    A. He paid her a large sum of money.
    B. He laughed and said he would deny it, that no one would believe a child.
    C. He convinced her that it was her fault, and that she had willingly participated.
    D. He threatened to kill Bailey if she told anyone.

Caged Bird Multiple Choice Questions Chapters 13-17

1. Which of the following did **not** happen to Mr. Freeman?
    A. He was sentenced to one year and one day in jail.
    B. He was severely beaten by the other inmates.
    C. His lawyer got him released the day of the trial.
    D. His body was found, apparently kicked to death.

2. What happened to Marguerite as a result of the experience?
    A. She stopped talking to everyone except Bailey. She thought that if she talked to anyone, that person might die, too.
    B. She got very wild, and started taking dangerous risks.
    C. She locked herself in a dark room and refused to come out.
    D. She screamed every time a man came near her.

3. What happened to Bailey and Marguerite after the doctor said she was healed?
    A. They went to live in Los Angeles with their father.
    B. They were sent up North to a boarding school.
    C. They were sent back to Stamps to live with Momma.
    D. They went to live with Grandmother Baxter.

4. Who took an interest in Marguerite, gave her books and told her to read them aloud, and to memorize a poem? Marguerite felt that this person liked and respected her.
    A. It was Miss McElroy.
    B. It was Mrs. Johnson.
    C. It was Miss Potter.
    D. It was Mrs. Flowers.

5. Why did Momma beat Marguerite and Bailey?
    A. She thought they were talking about sex and that was a forbidden subject.
    B. Momma overheard Marguerite using a phrase that she felt was blasphemous.
    C. She thought Marguerite was making fun of her by only talking to Bailey.
    D. They were singing. Singing was only allowed in church.

6. How did Marguerite feel about Mrs. Cullinan shortening her name to Mary?
    A. She liked the new "whitefolk" name.
    B. She didn't care one way or another.
    C. She didn't like it at all.
    D. She accepted it because it was better than being called a racial epithet.

7. How did Marguerite get out of working for Mrs. Cullinan?
    A. She spilled lemonade all over the guests.
    B. She went out and found another job that paid more.
    C. She pretended to be sick.
    D. She dropped some of Mrs. Cullinan's favorite china pieces.

8. Why had Bailey stayed out so late when he went to the movies?
    A. He had a secret girlfriend and he met her after the movie.
    B. He got in a fight and was trying to clean himself up first.
    C. He had a night job and didn't want anyone to know about it.
    D. One of the actresses resembled his mother. He stayed and watched the movie twice.

Caged Bird Multiple Choice Questions Chapters 18-21

1. True or False: The author believes that poor people attribute their existence and future to divine intervention. As people become more affluent, God descends in responsibility for their lives.
    A. True
    B. False

2. What "revolutionary action" took place at the revival?
    A. The preacher invited the women and girls to stand at the altar with him. Females had never before been allowed to do this.
    B. The preacher asked all of the ministers to cooperate in referring the newly saved sinners to the church of their choice.
    C. The preacher collected a general admission fee instead of relying on passing a collection plate.
    D. The preacher called for the Black communities to stand up against oppression.

3. What sport were the customers listening to on the radio when the Black contestant was declared world champion?
    A. It was baseball.
    B. It was tennis.
    C. It was boxing.
    D. It was auto racing.

4. How did Marguerite become friends with Louise Kendricks?
    A. They met in school while working together on a project.
    B. Louise came into the Store a lot to buy groceries for the family.
    C. Louise had a crush on Bailey, but then began to like Marguerite as a friend.
    D. They met in a grove of trees while attending the summer picnic.

5. What did Marguerite learn from Louise?
    A. She learned about the famous Black writer of the day.
    B. She learned to speak French.
    C. Marguerite learned what girls giggled about.
    D. She learned how to climb trees.

6. Who is being described here? Bailey had his first sexual experience with her. He stole candy from the store to please her. After a few months, she ran off with a railroad porter. Bailey became uncommunicative after she left. He and Marguerite had one brief conversation about her, and then never mentioned her again.
    A. It was Joyce.
    B. It was Janaice.
    C. It was Janelle.
    D. It was Jolene.

Caged Bird Multiple Choice Questions Chapters 22-24

1. How did Marguerite feel about the ghost stories that the customers told in the Store?
    A. She enjoyed them.
    B. She hated and dreaded them.

2. True or False: Marguerite finally realized the grim reality of death at Mrs. Taylor's funeral.
    A. True
    B. False

3. How did Momma interpret Mr. Taylor's vision/dream of his dead wife?
    A. She said he should donate money to build an orphanage in the town.
    B. She said Mrs. Taylor was happily taking care of all of the children in heaven.
    C. She said he should teach a Sunday School class and have a boy help on the farm.
    D. She said it was Mrs. Taylor's way of apologizing to him for leaving him all alone.

4. Why did Marguerite receive presents from Momma, Bailey, Louise, and others?
    A. She had received a scholarship to a Black high school in another town.
    B. She was graduating at the top of her eighth grade class.
    C. She was to be the salutatorian at the graduation.
    D. She had been voted "Most Likely to Succeed."

5. What happened at graduation that gave Marguerite a presentiment of worse things to come?
    A. They heard gunshots off in the distance as the ceremony started.
    B. There was a fierce storm, with a lot of thunder and lightening.
    C. Some of the local "powhitetrash" had vandalized the school.
    D. They were not allowed to sing the Black National Anthem, as they had rehearsed.

6. Describe the graduation speaker.
    A. He was the president of Tuskeegee University.
    B. She was a Civil Rights activist who was trying to get the schools integrated.
    C. He was a white man from Texarkana.
    D. He was a former student who was now on the football team at Arkansas A&M.

7. True or False: The graduation speech made Marguerite angry and sick at heart.
    A. True
    B. False

8. What happened after the speaker left?
    A. The class valedictorian led them in singing the Black National Anthem.
    B. They all started dancing.
    C. Some of the students were crying, but others were just very silent.
    D. They went on with the rest of the ceremony and forgot about the speaker.

9. True or False: The white dentist agreed to treat Marguerite as a favor to Momma.
    A. True
    B. False

10. What favor had Momma done for Dr. Lincoln?
    A. She had taken care of his children when his wife died.
    B. She had kept a local group of roughnecks from damaging his property.
    c. She special-ordered all of his favorite foods.
    D. Momma had lent him money, interest free, during the Depression.

Caged Bird Multiple Choice Questions Chapters 25-29

1. What did Maya Angelou think was the real reason Momma took her and Bailey to live in California with their parents?
    A. She thought that Momma knew she was getting old and might not be alive much longer.
    B. She thought it was because of the incident when Bailey saw a dead colored man, and helped take his body into calaboose for the white sheriff.
    C. She thought (and wanted to believe) that her parents had sent for them.
    D. She thought that Momma knew they would have more opportunities in a more urban environment.

2. What was the enigma of which Maya Angelou spoke?
    A. It was good vs. evil.
    B. It was suffering on Earth to receive a reward in Heaven.
    C. It was inequality and hate.
    D. It was determining which course of action was really the correct one.

3. What was the secret world given to Marguerite by Mrs. Flowers?
    A. It was gardening.
    B. It was meditation.
    C. It was optimism.
    D. It was books.

4. True or False: Bailey and Marguerite thought their mother's nervousness on the drive from Los Angeles to San Francisco made her seem more human to them.
    A True
    B. False

5. How did Bailey and Marguerite learn there were other people in the world?
    A. They were in a multi-racial high school.
    B. They watched a lot of television.
    C. They learned it through food. Their mother took them to many ethnic restaurants.
    D. They read a lot of books and magazines.

6. Which of the following does not describe Vivian Baxter's personality?
    A. She was jolly at times.
    B. She was merciful.
    C. She was quick-tempered.
    D. She was passionate.

7. What two events happened at this time in Marguerite's life?
   A. She sold her first story to a magazine, and moved to her own apartment..
   B. She fell in love for the first time and joined the ROTC.
   C. She failed a class for the first time, and changed her religion.
   D. The United States declared war on Japan, and her mother married Mr. Clidell.

8. What happened to the population of San Francisco's Fillmore district during the early months of World War II?
   A. It became less Asian and more Negro.
   B. It was taken over by the Navy for use as quarters for the sailors.
   C. It got run-down because the city didn't have the money for repairs.
   D. The property was bought up by rich white investors.

9. Which of the following does **not** describe Miss Kirwin, the teacher at George Washington High School?
   A. Miss Kirwin was in love with information.
   B. She was stimulating instead of intimidating.
   C. She was the only Black teacher at the school.
   D. She treated all of the students with respect.

10. Who is the author describing? ". . . that man who is offered only the crumbs from his country's table but by ingenuity and courage is able to take for himself a Lucullan feast."
    A. She is describing the black businessman.
    B. She is describing the hero of the Black ghetto.
    C. She is describing share-croppers in the South.
    D. She is describing the main character in a novel she was writing.

Caged Bird Multiple Choice Questions Chapters 30-33

1. Why did Marguerite go to Southern California?
    A. She wanted to go to school there.
    B. She was spending the summer with Daddy Bailey.
    C. She had a fight with her mother and moved in with her father out of spite.
    D. She wanted to go to Hollywood and become an actress.

2. True or False: Marguerite and Dolores became good friends.
    A. True
    B. False

3. True or False: On their trip to Mexico, Marguerite discovered that under his facade, her father was lonely and constantly searching for his place in the world.
    A. True
    B. False

4. What happened to her father while they were at the Mexican bar?
    A. He won a lot of money playing pool.
    B. He got into a fight with a few Mexican men and was thrown in a Mexican jail.
    C. He got drunk, went off with a Mexican woman, and was brought back to his car.
    D. He got a severe case of food poisoning and was very ill for two days.

5. True or False: Marguerite and Daddy Bailey left Mexico on two mules.
    A. True
    B. False

6. What was Marguerite's father's reaction when he found out she had a car accident?
    A. He laughed and said that experience was the best teacher.
    B. He told her shy would have to stay with him and get a job to pay for the damages.
    C. He said he was glad she was safe, that the car didn't matter.
    D. He commented that he didn't know she could drive, and asked if she liked his car.

7. Who had a fight?
    A. Daddy Bailey and one of his friends had a fight.
    B. Marguerite and her father had a fight.
    C. Marguerite and Dolores had a fight.
    D. Dolores and Vivian Baxter had a fight.

8. Marguerite spent the next month living in an abandoned car in a junkyard.
    A. True
    B. False

9. Who, according to the author, "were entangled in the Oedipal skein?"
    A. Bailey and Mother
    B. Dolores and Daddy Bailey
    C. herself and Daddy Clidell
    D. Mother and Daddy Bailey

10. What did Bailey do?
    A. He went away to college.
    B. He got a job in the rackets with Daddy Clidell.
    C. He went to work on the Southern Pacific Railroad.
    D. He went to live with Daddy Bailey.

Caged Bird Multiple Choice Questions Chapters 34-36

1. What job did Marguerite get?
    A. She got a job in a play in the theater district.
    B. She got a job as a writer with the local newspaper.
    C. She became the first Negro to work on the San Francisco streetcars.
    D. She became a tour guide at the art museum in Golden Gate Park.

2. How does Maya Angelou describe the change in her when the spring classes began?
    A. She was "aware of being aware."
    B. She was "ignorant of being ignorant ."
    C. She was "in love with life and love itself."
    D. She was "angry in a way I had never been angry before."

3. Which of the following forces did **not** assault the young Black female?
    A. the common forces of nature
    B. masculine prejudice
    C. white illogical hate
    D. jealousy

4. Of whom is the author speaking? It is "an inevitable outcome of the struggle won by survivors."
    A. the adult Black male
    B. the adult Black female
    C. the women of all races who worked during World War II.
    D. any oppressed minority

5. What new idea did Marguerite have as a result of reading *The Well of Loneliness?*
    A. She wanted to go to college and become a writer.
    B. She wanted to become a missionary.
    C. She thought she was a lesbian.
    d. She became obsessed with death.

6. True or False: Mother respond to Marguerite's questions about her body by laughing and telling her she should have figured out the answers to those questions long ago.
    A. True
    B. False

7. What was Marguerite's solution to her still-present concern over her sexual preferences?
   A. She went to the library to do some reading.
   B. She decided she would wait until she was older to think about it.
   C. She wrote a letter to her old friend, Louise.
   D. She decided she needed a boyfriend.

8. How did Marguerite become pregnant?
   A. She seduced a boy in the neighborhood.
   B. She went to a party, got drunk, and one of the boys took advantage of her.
   C. She was attacked by one of her mother's friends.
   D. She wanted to trap her boyfriend into marrying her, so she got pregnant on purpose.

9. How did her parents find out?
   A. The school nurse called them.
   B. Her pastor told them.
   C. She wrote them a letter.
   D. Her mother could tell that her shape was changing.

10. How did Maya Angelou react to her son after they came home from the hospital?
    A. She was a confident and took over all motherhood duties.
    B. She was unsure of herself, afraid she would hurt him.
    C. She was depressed and not able to care for him.
    D. She asked her mother to raise him.

ANSWER KEY MULTIPLE CHOICE QUIZ/STUDY GUIDE QUESTIONS
I Know Why The Caged Bird Sings

Chapters 1-6
1. C.
2. A.
3. B. False
4. D.
5. A. True
6. C.
7. B.
8. D.
9. B.
10. A.

Chapters 7-12
1. A.
2. C.
3. B.
4. A. True
5. D.
6. C.
7. B. False
8. D.

Chapters 13-17
1. B.
2. A.
3. C.
4. D.
5. B.
6. C.
7. D.
8. D.

Chapters 18-21
1. A. True
2. B.
3. C.
4. D.
5. C.
6. A.

Chapters 22-24
1. B.
2. A. True
3. C.
4. B.
5. D.
6. C.
7. A. True
8. A.
9. B. False
10. D.

Chapters 25-29
1. B.
2. C.
3. D.
4. A. True
5. C.
6. B.
7. D.
8. A.
9. C.
10. B.

Chapters 30-33
1. B.
2. B. False
3. A. True
4. C.
5. B. False
6. D.
7. C.
8. A. True
9. A.
10. C.

Chapters 34-36
1. C.
2. A.
3. D.
4. B.
5. C.
6. B. False
7. D.
8. A.
9. C.
10. B.

PREREADING VOCABULARY WORKSHEETS

Caged Bird Vocabulary Chapters 1-6
Introduction Part I: Using Prior Knowledge and Context Clues
Below are the sentences in which the vocabulary words appear in the text. Read the sentence. Use any clues you can find in the sentence combined with your prior knowledge, and write what you think the underlined words mean on the lines provided.

1. The dress I wore was lavender *taffeta*, and each time I breathed it rustled.

   _____

2. . . . and *troubadours* . . . leaned across its benches and sang their sad songs of The Brazos while they played juice harps and cigar-box guitars.

   _____

3. If he prophesied that the cotton in today's field was going to be *sparse* and stick to the bolls like glue, every listener would grunt a hearty agreement.

   _____

4. I was told even by my fellow Blacks that my *paranoia* was embarrassing.

   _____

5. She seemed to hold no *rancor* against the baby sitter.

   _____

6. His *nonchalance* was meant to convey his authority and power over even dumb animals.

   _____

7. A near *anachronism* in Stamps.

   _____

8. All adults had to be addressed as Mister, Missus, Miss, Auntie, Cousin, . . . and a thousand other *appellations* indicating familial relationship and the lowliness of the addressor.

   _____

9. In the Christian Methodist Episcopal Church the children's section was on the right, cater-corner from the pew that held those *ominous* women called the Mothers of the Church.

   _____

10. I'll never know what might have happened, because magically the *pandemonium* spread.

    _____

Part II: Determining the Meaning   Match the vocabulary words to their dictionary definitions.

___ 1.	taffeta	A.	extreme, irrational distrust of others
___ 2.	troubadours	B.	wild uproar or noise
___ 3.	sparse	C.	names, titles, or designations
___ 4.	paranoia	D.	a crisp fabric with a slight sheen
___ 5.	rancor	E.	menacing; threatening
___ 6.	nonchalance	F.	cool indifference
___ 7.	anachronism	G.	strolling minstrels
___ 8.	appellations	H.	out of proper or chronological order
___ 9.	ominous	I.	occurring at widely spaced intervals
___ 10.	pandemonium	J.	bitter, long-lasting resentment

Caged Bird Vocabulary Chapters 7-12

Introduction Part I: Using Prior Knowledge and Context Clues
Below are the sentences in which the vocabulary words appear in the text. Read the sentence. Use any clues you can find in the sentence combined with your prior knowledge, and write what you think the underlined words mean on the lines provided.

1. In fact, even in their absence they could not be spoken of too harshly unless we used the *sobriquet* "They."

   _____

2. He had the air of a man who did not believe what he heard or what he himself was saying. He was the first *cynic* I had met.

   _____

3. St. Louis teachers . . . talked down to their students from the lofty heights of education and white folks' *enunciation*. They . . . all sounded like my father with their *ers* and *errers*.

   _____

4. One of their more *flamboyant* escapades has become a proud family legend.

   _____

5. A natural comedian, he never waited for the laugh that he knew must follow his *droll* statements.

   _____

6. He would pretend at first not to see us, but with the *deftness* of a cat he would catch the ball.

   _____

7. Bailey persisted in calling her Mother Dear until the circumstance of *proximity* softened the phrase's formality to "Muh Dear," and finally to "M'Deah."

   _____

8. The weight of appreciation and the threat, which was never spoken, of a return to Momma were burdens that clogged my childish wits into *impassivity.*

___

9. He took his dinner off the stove where she had carefully covered it and which she had *admonished* us not to bother.

___

10. After he left the room I thought about telling Mother that I hadn't peed in the bed, but then if she asked me what happened I'd have to tell her about Mr. Freeman holding me, and that wouldn't do. It was the same old *quandary*.

___

Part II: Determining the Meaning   Match the vocabulary words to their dictionary definitions.

____ 1. sobriquet   A. one who believes others are selfish
____ 2. cynic   B. quickness; skillfulness
____ 3. enunciation   C. a state of uncertainty or perplexity
____ 4. flamboyant   D. gently reproved
____ 5. droll   E. amusingly odd
____ 6. deftness   F. closeness
____ 7. proximity   G. highly elaborate; showy
____ 8. impassivity   H. an affectionate nickname
____ 9. admonished   I. revealing no emotion
____ 10. quandary   J. pronounciation; articulation

Caged Bird Vocabulary Chapters 13-17

Introduction Part I: Using Prior Knowledge and Context Clues
Below are the sentences in which the vocabulary words appear in the text. Read the sentence. Use any clues you can find in the sentence combined with your prior knowledge, and write what you think the underlined words mean on the lines provided.

1. There is nothing more appalling than a constantly *morose* child.

   _____

2. It takes the human voice to *infuse* them with the shades of deeper meaning.

   _____

3. The three of us knelt as she began, "Our Father, you know the *tribulations* of your humble servant."

   _____

4. When I told her that in Stamps my grandmother had owned the only Negro general merchandise store . . . she exclaimed, "Why, you were a *debutante*!"

   _____

5. I thought of myself as hanging in the Store, a *mote* imprisoned on a shaft of sunlight.

   _____

6. One year later he did catch a freight, but because of his youth and the *inscrutable* ways of fate, he didn't find California and his Mother Dear-he got stranded in Baton Rouge, Louisiana, for two weeks.

   _____

Chapters 13-17 Part II: Determining the Meaning
Match the vocabulary words to their dictionary definitions.

____ 1. morose   A. difficult to understand
____ 2. infuse   B. sufferings
____ 3. tribulations   C. gloomy
____ 4. debutante   D. a very small particle; a speck.
____ 5. mote   E. a young woman entering society
____ 6. inscrutable   F. to fill with something

Caged Bird Vocabulary Chapters 18-21

Introduction Part I: Using Prior Knowledge and Context Clues
Below are the sentences in which the vocabulary words appear in the text. Read the sentence. Use any clues you can find in the sentence combined with your prior knowledge, and write what you think the underlined words mean on the lines provided.

1. Their shoulders drooped even as they laughed, and when they put their hands on their hips in a show of *jauntiness*, the palms slipped the thighs as if the pants were waxed.

   _____

2. I find it interesting that the meanest life, the poorest existence, is attributed to God's will, but as human beings become more affluent. as their living standard and style begin to ascend the material scale, God descends the scale of responsibility at a *commensurate* speed.

   _____

3. The idea came to me that my people may be a race of *masochists* and that not only was it our fate to live the poorest, roughest life but that we liked it like that.

   _____

4. The impermanence of a collapsible church added to the *frivolity*, and their eyes flashed and winked and the girls giggled little silver drops in the dusk while the boys postured and swaggered and pretended not to notice.

   _____

5. To small children, though, the idea of praising God in a tent was confusing, to say the least. It seemed somehow *blasphemous*.

   _____

6. The latter were looked upon with some suspicion because they were so loud and *raucous* in their services.

   _____

7. Their explanation that "the Good Book say, 'Make a joyful noise unto the Lord, and be exceedingly glad'" did not in the least minimize the *condescension* of their fellow Christians.

8. However, in the *ecumenical* light of the summer picnic every true baking artist could reveal her prize to the delight and criticism of the town.

9. I had been thinking of yesterday's plain invitation and the *expeditious* way Louise and I took care of it.

10. Unfortunately the situation was so wonderful to me that each time I saw Tommy I melted in delicious giggles and was unable to form a *coherent* sentence.

Part II: Determining the Meaning   Match the vocabulary words to their dictionary definitions.

___ 1. jauntiness   A. of the same size or proportion
___ 2. commensurate   B. acting in a patronizingly superior way
___ 3. masochists   C. promoting unity among religions
___ 4. frivolity   D. sticking together
___ 5. blasphemous   E. having a buoyant or self-confident air
___ 6. raucous   F. speaking irreverently of a sacred being
___ 7. condescension   G. those who enjoy being mistreated
___ 8. ecumenical   H. done with speed and efficiency
___ 9. expeditious   I. rough-sounding
___ 10. coherent   J. silliness

Caged Bird Vocabulary Chapters 22-24

Introduction Part I: Using Prior Knowledge and Context Clues
Below are the sentences in which the vocabulary words appear in the text. Read the sentence. Use any clues you can find in the sentence combined with your prior knowledge, and write what you think the underlined words mean on the lines provided.

1. But on that *onerous* day, oppressed beyond relief, my own mortality was borne in upon me on sluggish tides of doom.

   _____

2. The cheeks had fallen back to the ears and a *solicitous* mortician had put lipstick on the black mouth.

   _____

3. Youth and social approval allied themselves with me and we *trammeled* memories of slights and insults.

   _____

4. But since he had called our names at the beginning of the service we were *mollified*.

   _____

5. The ugliness they left was *palpable*.

   _____

6. Elouise, the daughter of the Baptist minister, recited "Invictus," and I could have cried at the *impertinence* of "I am the master of my fate, I am the captain of my soul."

   _____

7. Henry had been a good student in *elocution*.

   _____

8. I had been listening and silently *rebutting* each sentence with my eyes closed.

9. The Angel of the candy counter had found me out at last, and was exacting *excruciating* penance for all the stolen Milky Ways, Mounds, Mr. Goodbars and Hersheys with Almonds.

10. Momma and her son laughed and laughed over the white man's evilness and her *retributive* sin.

Part II: Determining the Meaning   Match the vocabulary words to their dictionary definitions.

____ 1.	onerous	A.	expressing care or concern
____ 2.	solicitous	B.	public speaking
____ 3.	trammeled	C.	demanded in repayment
____ 4.	mollified	D.	boldness
____ 5.	palpable	E.	capable of being touched or felt
____ 6.	impertinence	F.	offering opposing evidence
____ 7.	elocution	G.	calmed; soothed
____ 8.	rebutting	H.	troublesome
____ 9.	excruciating	I.	extremely painful
____ 10.	retributive	J.	restrained, restricted

Caged Bird Vocabulary Chapters 25-29

Introduction Part I: Using Prior Knowledge and Context Clues
Below are the sentences in which the vocabulary words appear in the text. Read the sentence. Use any clues you can find in the sentence combined with your prior knowledge, and write what you think the underlined words mean on the lines provided.

1. He was away in a mystery, locked in an *enigma* that young Southern Black boys start to unravel, from seven years old to death.

   _____

2. The Black newcomer had been recruited on the *desiccated* farm lands of Georgia and Mississippi by war-plant labor scouts.

   _____

3. & 4. The air of collective displacement, the impermanence of life in wartime and the *gauche* personalities of the more recent arrivals tended to *dissipate* my own sense of not belonging.

   _____

   _____

5. I understood the arrogance of the young sailors who marched the streets in *marauding* gangs, approaching every girl as if she were at best a prostitute and at worst an Axis agent bent on making the U.S.A. lose the war.

   _____

6. The undertone of fear that San Francisco would be bombed which was *abetted* by weekly air raid warnings, and civil defense drills in school, heightened my sense of belonging.

   _____

7. Native San Franciscans, possessive of the city, had to cope with an influx, not of awed respectful tourists but of raucous unsophisticated *provincials*.

   _____

8. My Miss Kirwin, who was a tall, *florid*, buxom lady with battleship gray hair, taught civics and current events.

_____

9. No *recriminations* lay hidden under the plain statement, now was there boasting when he said, "If I'm living a little better now, it's because I treat everybody right."

_____

10. Petty crimes embarrass the community and many white people wistfully wonder why Negroes don't rob more banks, *embezzle* more funds and employ graft in the unions.

_____

Part II: Determining the Meaning   Match the vocabulary words to their dictionary definitions.

_____ 1. enigma   A. to cause to lose irreversibly
_____ 2. desiccated   B. helped
_____ 3. gauche   C. rosy colored
_____ 4. dissipate   D. to take in violation of a trust
_____ 5. marauding   E. countercharges
_____ 6. abetted   F. unsophisticsted people
_____ 7. provincials   G. raiding to plunder
_____ 8. florid   H. lacking social polish
_____ 9. recriminations   I. something puzzling or inexplicable
_____ 10. embezzle   J. arid, dried out

Caged Bird Vocabulary Chapters 30-33

Introduction Part I: Using Prior Knowledge and Context Clues
Below are the sentences in which the vocabulary words appear in the text. Read the sentence. Use any clues you can find in the sentence combined with your prior knowledge, and write what you think the underlined words mean on the lines provided.

1. When I met Dolores she had all the poses of the black *bourgeoisie* without the material basis to support the postures.

   _____

2. I was asked, *cajoled*, then ordered to care for my room.

   _____

3. He seemed positively *diabolic* in his enjoyment of our discomfort.

   _____

4. Then I explained that I didn't like her because she was mean and petty and full of *pretense*.

   _____

5. Buoyed by the adrenaline that had flooded my brain as we careened down the mountainside, I had never felt better, and my father's snores cut through the *cacophony* of protestations outside my window.

   _____

6. Terror did not engulf me wholly, but crawled along my mind like a *tedious* paralysis.

   _____

7. I didn't expect or even need, now, his *approbation.*

   _____

8. He said he told her if the _laceration_ wasn't too deep he would be grateful if she treated it.

   _____

9. The _deferential_ tone heightened the content of his announcement.

   _____

10. Sailors and soldiers on their doom-lined road to war cracked windows and broke locks for blocks around, hoping to leave their imprint on a building or in the memory of a victim. A chance to be _perpetrated._

    _____

Part II: Determining the Meaning   Match the vocabulary words to their dictionary definitions.

____ 1.	bourgeoisie	A.	characteristic of the devil
____ 2.	cajoled	B.	the middle class
____ 3.	diabolic	C.	committed
____ 4.	pretense	D.	tiresome due to extreme slowness
____ 5.	cacophony	E.	false appearance
____ 6.	tedious	F.	a jagged, deep cut
____ 7.	approbation	G.	jarring, discordant sounds
____ 8.	laceration	H.	courteous, respectful
____ 9.	deferential	I.	urged gently
____ 10.	perpetrated	J.	warm approval, praise

Caged Bird Vocabulary Chapters 34-36

Introduction Part I: Using Prior Knowledge and Context Clues
Below are the sentences in which the vocabulary words appear in the text. Read the sentence. Use any clues you can find in the sentence combined with your prior knowledge, and write what you think the underlined words mean on the lines provided.

1. When I spoke in *supercilious* accents, and looked at the room as if I had an oil well in my backyard, my armpits were being pricked by millions of hot pointed needles.

   _____

2. The next three weeks were a honeycomb of determination with *apertures* for the days to go in and out.

   _____

3. Another time she reminded me that "God helps those who help themselves." She had a store of *aphorisms* which she dished out as the occasion demanded.

   _____

4. I only knew that one day, which was tiresomely like all the others before it, I sat in the Railway office, *ostensibly* waiting to be interviewed.

   _____

5. I had little time to wonder if I had won or not, for the standard questions reminded me of the necessity for *dexterous* lying.

   _____

6. They were, according to the book, disowned by their families, snubbed by their friends and *ostracized* from every society.

   _____

7. Had I been older I might have thought that I was moved by both an *esthetic* sense of beauty and the pure emotion of envy.

_____

8. I planned a chart for seduction with surprise as my opening *ploy*.

_____

9. One evening as I walked up the hill suffering from youth's vague *malaise* (there was simply nothing to do), the brother I had chosen came walking directly into my trap.

_____

10. I very nearly caught the essence of teenage *capriciousness* as I played the role.

_____

Part II: Determining the Meaning   Match the vocabulary words to their dictionary definitions.

_____ 1. supercilious   A. an action done to frustrate
_____ 2. apertures   B. impulsiveness
_____ 3. aphorisms   C. banished or excluded from a group
_____ 4. ostensibly   D. appearing as such
_____ 5. dexterous   E. openings
_____ 6. ostracized   F. general sense of depression
_____ 7. esthetic   G. showing haughty disdain
_____ 8. ploy   H. appreciating beauty
_____ 9. malaise   I. skillful
_____ 10. capriciousness   J. brief statements of principles

ANSWER KEY- VOCABULARY
I Know Why the Caged Bird Sings

Chapters 1-6
1. D
2. G
3. I
4. A
5. J
6. F
7. H
8. C
9. E
10. B

Chapters 7-12
1. H
2. A
3. J
4. G
5. E
6. B
7. F
8. I
9. D
10. C

Chapters 13-17
1. C
2. F
3. B
4. E
5. D
6. A

Chapters 18-21
1. E
2. A
3. G
4. J
5. F
6. I
7. B
8. C
9. H
10. D

Chapters 22-24
1. H
2. A
3. J
4. G
5. E
6. D
7. B
8. F
9. I
10. C

Chapters 25-29
1. I
2. J
3. H
4. A
5. G
6. B
7. F
8. C
9. E
10. D

Chapters 30-33
1. B
2. I
3. A
4. E
5. G
6. D
7. J
8. F
9. H
10. C

Chapters 34-36
1. G
2. E
3. J
4. D
5. I
6. C
7. H
8. A
9. F
10. B

DAILY LESSONS

LESSON ONE

Objective
1. To introduce the *I Know Why the Caged Bird Sings* unit
2. To distribute books and other related materials (study guides, reading assignments)
3. To relate students' prior knowledge to the new material
4. To preview the study questions for Chapters 1-6
5. To familiarize students with the vocabulary for Chapters 1-6

Activity #1

Ask students for a show of hands of those who have at some time in the past moved, changed schools or neighborhoods, or have gone to live with relatives other than their parents. Invite students to share their experiences as much as they care to.

You may also want to involve students in a discussion of racial prejudice, and provide some background on the prevailing racial climate in the United States at the time the book was written about (1931-1950.)

Tell students that the book they are about to read is an autobiography, written by the author about her life from the ages of three through sixteen. In this book she shares her experiences about living with various family members. She also makes observations about the disparities between Black and white lifestyles and outlooks.

Activity #2

Distribute the materials students will use in this unit. Explain in detail how students are to use these materials.

Study Guides Students should preview the study guide questions before each reading assignment to get a feeling for what events and ideas are important in that section. After reading the section, students will (as a class or individually) answer the questions to review the important events and ideas from that section of the book. Students should keep the study guides as study materials for the unit test.

Reading Assignment Sheet You need to fill in the reading assignment sheet to let students know when their reading has to be completed. You can either write the assignment sheet on a side blackboard or bulletin board and leave it there for students to see each day, or you can "ditto" copies for each student to have. In either case, you should advise students to become very familiar with the reading assignments so they know what is expected of them.

<u>Extra Activities Center</u> The resource sections of this unit contain suggestions for a library of related books and articles in your classroom as well as crossword and word search puzzles. Make an extra activities center in your room where you will keep these materials for students to use. (Bring the books and articles in from the library and keep several copies of the puzzles on hand). Explain to students that these materials are available for students to use when they finish reading assignments or other class work early.

<u>Books</u> Each school has its own rules and regulations regarding student use of school books. Advise students of the procedures that are normal for your school.

<u>Nonfiction Assignment Sheet</u>

Explain to students that they each are to read at least one nonfiction piece at some time during the unit. Students will fill out a nonfiction assignment sheet after completing the reading to help you (the teacher) evaluate their reading experiences and to help the students think about and evaluate their own reading experiences.

<u>Activity #3</u>

Do a group KWL Sheet with the students (form included.) Many students will know something aboutMaya Angelou and will have information to share. Put this information in the K column (what I know.) Ask students what they want to find out, and put it in the W column (what I want to find out.) Keep the sheet and refer back to it after reading the book, and complete the L column (what I learned.)

<u>Activity #4</u>

Show students how to preview the study questions and do the vocabulary work for Chapters 1-6 of *I Know Why the Caged Bird Sings*. If students do not finish this assignment during the class period, they should complete it prior to the next class meeting.

KWL *I Know why the Caged Bird Sings*

Directions: Before reading, think about what you already know about Maya Angelou and/or *I Know why the Caged Bird Sings*. Write the information in the K column. Think about what you would like to find out from reading the book. Write your questions in the W column. After you have read the book, use the L column to write the answers to your questions from the W column, and anything else you remember from the book.

K **What I Know**	**W** **What I Want to Find Out**	**L** **What I Learned**

NONFICTION ASSIGNMENT SHEET *I Know Why the Caged Bird Sings*

(To be completed after reading the required nonfiction article)

Name _____ Date _____ Class _____

Title of Nonfiction Read _____

Written By _____ Publication Date _____

I. Factual Summary: Write a short summary of the piece you read.

II. Vocabulary:
    1. With which vocabulary words in the piece did you encounter some degree of difficulty?

    2. How did you resolve your lack of understanding with these words?

III. Interpretation: What was the main point the author wanted you to get from reading his/her work?

IV. Criticism:
1. With which points of the piece did you agree or find easy to accept? Why?

2. With which points of the piece did you disagree or find difficult to believe? Why?

V. Personal Response: What do you think about this piece? OR How does this piece influence your ideas?

LESSON TWO

Objectives
    1. To read Chapters 1-6 orally
    2. To give students practice reading orally
    4. To evaluate students' oral reading

Activity

    Have students read Chapters 1-6 of *I Know Why the Caged Bird Sings* out loud in class. You probably know the best way to get readers with your class; pick students at random, ask for volunteers, or use whatever method works best for your group. If you have not yet completed an oral reading evaluation for your students for this marking period, this would be a good opportunity to do so. A form is included with this unit for your convenience. If students do not complete reading Chapters 1-6 in class, they should do so prior to your next class meeting.

LESSON THREE

Objectives
    1. To review the main ideas and events from Chapters 1-6
    2. To preview the study questions for Chapters 7-12
    3. To familiarize students with the vocabulary in Chapters 7-12
    4. To read Chapters 7-12

Activity #1

    Give students a few minutes to formulate answers for the study guide questions for Chapters 1-2, and then discuss the answers to the questions in detail. Write the answers on the board or overhead projector so students can have the correct answers for study purposes. Encourage students to take notes. If students have purchased their own copies of the book, suggest that they use highlighters in their books to indicate vocabulary words and the answers to study guide questions.

    Note: It is a good practice in public speaking and leadership skills for individual students to take charge of leading the discussions of the study questions. Perhaps a different student could go to the front of the class and lead the discussion each day that the study questions are discussed during this unit. Of course, the teacher should guide the discussion when appropriate and be sure to fill in any gaps the students leave.

Activity #2

    Give students about fifteen minutes to preview the study questions for Chapters 7-12 of *I Know Why the Caged Bird Sings* and do the related vocabulary work.

Activity #3

    Assign students to read Chapters 7-12 of *I Know Why the Caged Bird Sings* prior to your next class period. If there is time remaining in this period, students may begin reading silently.

ORAL READING EVALUATION *I Know Why the Caged Bird Sings*

Name_____Class_____Date_____- -

SKILL	EXCELLENT	GOOD	AVERAGE	FAIR	POOR
Fluency	5	4	3	2	1
Clarity	5	4	3	2	1
Audibility	5	4	3	2	1
Pronunciation	5	4	3	2	1
_____	5	4	3	2	1
_____	5	4	3	2	1

Total _____ Grade _____

Comments:

LESSON FOUR

Objectives
1. To check to see that students read Chapters 7-12 as assigned
2. To review the main ideas and events from Chapters 7-12
3. To preview the study questions for Chapters 13-17
4. To familiarize students with the vocabulary in Chapters 13-17
5. To read Chapters 13-17
6. To evaluate students' oral reading

Activity #1

Quiz--Distribute quizzes (multiple choice study questions for Chapters 7-12) and give students about ten minutes to complete them. Have students exchange papers. Grade the quizzes as a class. Collect the papers for recording the grades.

Activity #2

Give students about 15 minutes to preview the study questions for Chapters 13-17 and do the related vocabulary work.

Activity #3

Have students read Chapters 13-17 orally for the rest of the period. Continue the oral reading evaluations. If students do not complete reading these Chapters during this class period, they should do so prior to your next class meeting.

LESSON FIVE

Objectives
1. To give students the opportunity to practice writing an autobiography
2. To give the teacher an opportunity to evaluate each student's writing skills

Activity #1

Distribute Writing Assignment #1 and discuss the directions in detail. Allow the remaining class time for students to work on the assignment. Give students an additional two or three days to complete the assignment.

Activity #2

Distribute copies of the Writing Evaluation Form (included in this Unit Plan). Explain to students that during Lesson Nine you will be holding individual writing conferences about this writing assignment. Make sure they are familiar with the criteria on the Writing Evaluation Form.

WRITING ASSIGNMENT #1 *I Know Why the Caged Bird Sings*

PROMPT

I Know Why the Caged Bird Sings is an autobiography. It is the story of the early life of Maya Angelou as she remembers it. She includes character descriptions of the important people in her life, vivid descriptions of the places she lived, and details about the events that occurred. Most importantly, she offers an insight into her own reactions, thoughts, and feelings.

Your assignment is to write a brief autobiography.

PREWRITING

Ms. Angelou covered a span of about 13 years in her autobiography. Yours does not have to be this comprehensive. You may want to focus on one particularly interesting event or on the events of an entire year. It may help you to make a timeline of the significant events in your life. Then you can choosewhat you want to write about.

In the Acknowledgment in the front of the book, Ms. Angelou thanks her mother and brother for their assistance in helping her remember incidents from her early life. You may want to interview people who knew you as a young child. You should prepare a list of questions ahead of time for them to answer, and also be ready to listen to them reminisce. You may want to tape record the interviews so that you can listen to them again as you are writing.

Organize the events in a chronological order so that the reader can follow the events as they occurred in your life.

You may want to reread Chapters 1 and 2 of *I Know Why the Caged Bird Sings* to see how Ms. Angelou introduces herself to the reader.

DRAFTING

First, write a paragraph in which you introduce an important event in your life. Make sure you include background information about the setting (year, location) and the other people involved.

In the body of your autobiography, continue telling about the event or events, adding details about the other people involved. Make sure to include observations about your own thoughts and feelings.

Finally, write a concluding paragraph in which you talk abut the ways that the event/events you wrote about have influenced your life today.

PROOFREADING

When you finish the rough draft of your paper, ask another student to read it. After reading your rough draft, he/she should tell you what he/she liked best about your work, which parts were difficult to understand, and ways in which your work could be improved. Reread your paper considering your critic's comments, and make the corrections you think are necessary.

Do a final proofreading of your paper, double-checking your grammar, spelling, organization, and the clarity of your ideas.

WRITING EVALUATION FORM *I Know Why the Caged Bird Sings*

Name _____ Date _____ Class _____

Writing Assignment #____ for *I Know Why the Caged Bird Sings*

Circle One For Each Item:

Introduction	excellent	good	fair	poor
Body Paragraphs	excellent	good	fair	poor
Summary	excellent	good	fair	poor
Grammar	excellent	good	fair	poor (errors noted)
Spelling	excellent	good	fair	poor (errors noted)
Punctuation	excellent	good	fair	poor (errors noted)
Legibility	excellent	good	fair	poor (errors noted)

Strengths:

Weaknesses:

Comments/Suggestions:

LESSON SIX

Objectives
    1. To review the main ideas in Chapters 13-17
    2. To preview the study questions and vocabulary for Chapters 18-21
    3. To read Chapters 18-21 silently

Activity #1

    Ask students to get out their books and some paper (not their study guides.) Tell students to write down ten questions and answers which cover the main events and ideas in Chapters 13-17. Discuss the students' questions and answers orally, making a list on the board of the questions with brief responses. Put a star next to the students' questions and answers that are essentially the same as the study guide questions. Be sure that all the study guide questions are answered.

Activity #2

    Tell students to do the prereading and reading work for Chapters 18-21 prior to your next class meeting. Students may use the remainder of this class period to begin working on this assignment.

LESSON SEVEN

Objectives
    1. To review the main ideas and events of Chapters 18-21
    2. To check to see that the students did the reading assignment
    3. To assign the pre-reading, vocabulary, and reading work for Chapters 22-24

Activity #1

    Give students a quiz on Chapters 18-21. Use either the short answer or multiple choice form of the study guide questions as a quiz so that in discussing the answers to the quiz you also answer the study guide questions. Collect the papers for grade recording.

Activity #2

    Tell students that prior to the next lesson they must have completed the pre-reading, vocabulary and reading work for Chapters 22-24. Give them the rest of the class period to work on this assignment. You may want to allow students who finish early to go to the library and find information for their nonfiction assignments.

LESSON EIGHT

<u>Objectives</u>
     1. To review the main ideas and events from Chapters 22-24
     2. To introduce Writing Assignment #2

<u>Activity #1</u>
     Review the study questions from Chapters 22-24.

<u>Activity #2</u>
     Distribute Writing Assignment #2. Discuss the directions in detail and give students ample time to complete the assignment. Give students the rest of this period to begin working on Writing Assignment #2, to do more research for the Nonfiction Reading Assignment, or to catch up on their reading.

WRITING ASSIGNMENT #2 *I Know Why the Caged Bird Sings*

PROMPT

You are applying for a job. The first thing you need to do is write a resume. A resume is a brief summary of your qualifications and work experiences. If you have never seen a resume, ask someone who has one to show it to you. There are books in the library that have sample resumes. A sample resume is also provided for you. Note: The information on the resume is only provided as an outline for the kind of information you should include. It is purely a work of fiction. It does not reflect the actual experiences that are necessary to becoming a lifeguard.

PREWRITING

The resume should have several parts. In the first part, list your personal information (name, address, telephone number). Next, write a one or two sentence summary about the job you desire. In the next section, list your educational experience. You may want to include your grade point average, but it is not required. Next briefly describe your three or four best skills or talents. Then list any work experience that you have had. Include volunteer experiences. Tell a little bit about the kinds of responsibilities you had, and what your achievements were. Next list any clubs or organizations to which you belong. You may include a section describing your interests and hobbies, especially if they are related to the job you want. You may include church-related activities. You do not have to mention your religion if you don't want to. Saying "church-related activities" is sufficient.

Before you start writing, you need to gather all of the necessary information. Make sure that the names, addresses, and other information are correct.

DRAFTING

A resume is different from an expository paper. You will not write in paragraphs, but rather in a modified list form.

When you list your education and work experiences, start with your most recent one and work backwards. Your earliest school and first job should be the last ones in those sections.

If you are handwriting your resume, keep it to two pages. If you are typing or using a computer, the resume should be only one page long.

PROMPT

When you finish the rough draft of your resume, ask another student to look at it. After reading your rough draft, he/she will tell you what he/she liked best about your work, which parts were not clear, and ways in which your work could be improved. Reread your resume considering your critic's comments, and make the corrections you think are necessary.

PROOFREADING

Do a final proofreading of your resume, double-checking your grammar, spelling, organization, and the clarity of your ideas.

WRITING ASSIGNMENT #2 *I Know Why the Caged Bird Sings.*
SAMPLE RESUME

Your Name
Address
Telephone Number 1-(area code) number

Career Objective

    Lifeguard/Swimming Instructor

Education

    Central High School, City, State, 19-- -present. Currently a (freshman, etc.)
    Oak Street Middle School, 19-- to 19--
    Main Street Elementary School, City, State, 19-- to 19--

Primary Skills

    Earned Water Safety Certificate, Scout Program, 1991
    Certified Red Cross Lifeguard, 1991
    Passed Red Cross Babysitting class, 1989

Work Experience

    Lifeguard, York City Pool, Summers 1993 and 1994
    Babysitting for families with from one to six children since 1990
    Volunteer lifeguard/childcare for various church activities, 1989-present

Memberships

    Church Youth Group, 1991-present. President, 1995-96
    National Honor Society
    American Red Cross
    (Boy, Girl) Scouts of America 1986-1994

Hobbies

    Reading, swimming, hiking, tennis

References are available on request.

LESSON NINE

Objectives

    1. To have students revise their first writing assignment papers

    2. To give students time to work on their other reading and writing assignments

Activity #1

    Call students to your desk (or some other private area) to discuss their papers from Writing Assignment #1. Use the completed Writing Evaluation Form as a basis for your critique.

Activity #2

    Students should use this period (when they are not conferencing with you) to work on Writing Assignment #2, revisions of Writing Assignment #1, or their Nonfiction reading assignment.

LESSON TEN

Objectives

    1. To do the prereading and vocabulary work for Chapters 25-29

    2. To read Chapters 25-29 aloud with a partner

    3. To review the main ideas and events from Chapters 25-29

Activity #1

    Distribute copies of the vocabulary worksheet and give students about ten minutes to complete it.

Activity #2

    Go over the Study Guide questions for Chapters 25-29.

Activity #3

    Explain to the students that they will be doing partner reading. Assign partners, or let the students choose their own (whichever works best for your class.) Students will take turns reading aloud in a low voice to each other.

Activity #4

    Allow student partners to work together to answer the Study Guide questions. Review the answers with the students.

LESSON ELEVEN

Objectives
1. To do the prereading and vocabulary work for Chapters 30-33
2. To become familiar with the Spanish terms used in Chapter 30
2. To listen to the teacher read Chapters 30-33
3. To review the main ideas and events from Chapters 30-33

Activity #1

Distribute copies of the vocabulary worksheet for Chapters 30-33. Give students about ten minutes to complete the work.

Activity #2

Go over the Study Guide questions with the students. Tell them that since they will be listening to you read aloud today, they should take notes while they are listening.

Activity #3

Begin reading aloud to the students. Encourage them to follow along in their books. Explain the Spanish phrases as you come to them in Chapter 30. If one of the students speaks Spanish, ask him/her to pronounce the phrases correctly and have the rest of the class repeat them. Help students determine the meanings of the phrases through the context of the story. A translation of each phrase is also provided here for you.

adios--good-bye
bonita--pretty
esposita--little wife
cantina--public-house, saloon, bar
¿Cómo está usted?--How are you?
chicharrones -- cracking, fried lard left in the pan
¿Dónde está mi padre?--Where is my father?
¿Dónde vas?--Where are you going?
Yo voy por ventilarme. --*(literally, I am going to air myself out.) She probably wanted to
            say that she was going out for some fresh air.*
Si, si--yes, yes
Gracias--Thank you
Pasa--Go ahead, pass
policías--police
Joven--young
Borracho--drunk
pobrecita--poor little thing, poor little girl
¿Qué tiene? --What do you have?
¿Qué pasa?--What's going on?, What happened?

LESSON TWELVE

Objectives
    1. To preview the study questions and vocabulary for Chapters 34-36
    2. To silently read Chapters 34-36
    3. To predict the answers to the Study Guide questions
    3. To discuss the main ideas and events from Chapters 34-36

Activity #1
    Distribute copies of the vocabulary worksheet for Chapters 34-36. Give students about ten minutes to complete the work.

Activity #2
    Distribute copies of the Multiple Choice/Quiz Study Guide questions. Encourage students to make predictions about the answers by circling or underlining the answer they think is correct.

Activity #3
    Have the students read the chapters silently and compare their original predictions with the actual answers to the multiple choice questions.

LESSON THIRTEEN

Objective
    To discuss *I Know Why the Caged Bird Sings* on interpretive and critical levels

Activity #1
    Choose the questions from the Extra Discussion Questions/Writing Assignments which seem most appropriate for your students. A class discussion of these questions is most effective of students have been given the opportunity to formulate answers to the questions prior to the discussion. To this end, you may either have all the students formulate answers to all the questions, divide your class into groups and assign one or more questions to each group, or you could assign one question to each student in your class. The option you choose will make a difference in the amount of class time needed for this activity.

Activity #2
    After students have had ample time to formulate answers to the questions, begin your class discussion of the questions and the ideas presented by the questions. Be sure students take notes during the discussion so they have information to study for the unit test.

EXTRA WRITING ASSIGNMENT/DISCUSSION QUESTIONS
I Know Why the Caged Bird Sings

Interpretation

1. From what point of view is the book written? How does this affect our understanding of the story?

2. How does Ms. Angelou's perspective influence the autobiography?

3. What insights into the life of the American rural Black community does the author provide?

4. Why do you think Maya kept her pregnancy a secret from everyone?

5. To what is Ms. Angelou referring in the dedication of the book?

6. Why do you think the graduating students were kept from singing the Black National Anthem?

7. Which of the events in the book seemed to have been the most positive influences on Ms. Angelou?

8. Which of the events in the book seemed to have been the most negative influences on Ms. Angelou?

9. The title of the book comes from the poem "Sympathy" by Paul Lawrence Dunbar." Read the poem and discuss its relevance, to this autobiography.

Critical

10. Discuss the role of imagery in *I Know Why the Caged Bird Sings*.

11. Discuss the role of metaphor in *I Know Why the Caged Bird Sings*.

12. Do you agree or disagree with Ms. Angelou's observation about differences among places? "What sets one Southern town apart from another, or from a Northern town or hamlet, or city high-rise? The answer must be the experience shared between the unknowing majority (it) and the knowing minority (you)."

13. What do you think Maya Angelou learned form each of the important people in her life?

14. Which of the personalities in the book seemed to be the most fully developed?

15. Which of the presonalities in the book seemed to be the least developed?

Personal Response

16. Did you enjoy reading *I Know Why the Caged Bird Sings*? Why or why not?

17 Have you read any other autobiographies? How were they like this one? How were they different?

18 How did you feel about Vivian Baxter and Bailey Johnson as parents?

19 Have you read any other works by Maya Angelou? Did you like them? If you have read several, which was your favorite?

20 How does your own ethnic background influence your understanding/interpretation of *I Know Why the Caged Bird Sings*?

21. What other title would you choose for this book? Why?

QUOTATIONS

Discuss the significance of the following quotations.

1. "I was going to look like one of the sweet little white girls who were everybody's dream of what was right with the world."

2. "Because I was really white and because a cruel fairy stepmother , who was understandably jealous of my beauty, had turned me into a too-big Negro girl, with nappy black hair, broad feet and a space between her teeth that would hold a number two pencil."

3. "If growing up is painful for the Southern Black girl, being aware of her displacement is the rust on the razor that threatens the throat."

4. "Years later I discovered that the United States had been crossed thousands of times by frightened Black children traveling alone to their newly affluent parents in Northern cities, or back to grandmothers in Southern towns when the urban North reneged on its economic promises."

5. "In later years I was to confront the stereotyped picture of gay song-singing cotton pickers with such inordinate rage that my paranoia was embarrassing. But I had seen the fingers cut by the mean little cotton bolls, and I had witnessed the backs and shoulders and arms and legs resisting any further demands."

6. "In cotton-picking time the late afternoons revealed the harshness of Black Southern life, which in the early morning had been softened by nature's blessing of grogginess, forgetfulness and the soft lamplight."

7. "But it was Shakespeare who said 'When in disgrace with fortune and men's eyes.' It was a state with which I felt myself most familiar. I pacified myself about his whiteness by saying that after all he had been dead so long it couldn't matter to anyone anymore."

8. "It seemed that the peace of a day's ending was an assurance that the covenant god made with children, Negroes and the crippled was still in effect."

9. " 'Annie, tell Willie he better lay low tonight. A crazy nigger messed with a white lady today. some of the boys'll be coming over here later.' Even after the slow drag of years, I remember the sense of fear which filled my mouth with hot, dry air, and made my body light."

10. "Of all the needs (there are none imaginary) a lonely child has, the one that must be satisfied, if there is going to be hope and a hope of wholeness, is the unshaking need for an unshakable God."

11. "Later he explained that when a person is beating you you should scream as loud as possible; maybe the whipper will become embarrassed or else some sympathetic soul might come to your rescue."

12. "She said that I must always be intolerant of ignorance but understanding of illiteracy. That some people, unable to go to school, were more educated and even more intelligent than college professors."

13. "I was liked, and what a difference it made. I was respected not as Mrs. Henderson's grandchild or Bailey's sister but for just being Marguerite Johnson."

14. "Children's talent to endure stems from their ignorance of alternatives."

15. "Every person I knew had a hellish horror of being 'called out of his name.' It was a dangerous practice to call a Negro anything that could be loosely construed as insulting because of the centuries of their having been called niggers, jigs, dinges, blackbirds, crows, boots and spooks."

16. "And it was funny to think of the whitefolks' not knowing that the woman they were adoring could be my mother's own, except that she was white and my mother was prettier. Much prettier."

17. "When they tried to smile to carry off their tiredness as if it was nothing, the body did nothing to help the mind's attempt at disguise. Their shoulders drooped even as they laughed, and when they put their hands on their hips in a show of jauntiness, the palms slipped the thighs as if the pants were waxed."

18. "It wouldn't do for a Black man and his family to be caught on a lonely country road on a night when Joe Louis had proved that we were the strongest people in the world."

19. "It was awful to be Negro and have no control over my life. It was brutal to be young and already trained to sit quietly and listen to charges brought against my color with no chance of defense."

20. "Oh, Black known and unknown poets, how often have your auctioned pains sustained us? Who will compute the lonely nights made less lonely by your songs, or by the empty pots made less tragic by your tales?"

21. "He was away in a mystery, locked in the enigma that young Southern Black boys start to unravel, start to *try* to unravel, from seven years old to death. The humorless puzzle of inequality and hate."

22. "He had told me once that 'all knowledge is spendable currency, depending on the market.' "

23. "The quality of strength lined with tenderness is an unbeatable combination, as are intelligence and necessity when unblunted by formal education."

24. "At fifteen life had taught me undeniably that surrender, in its place, was as honorable as resistance, especially if one had no choice."

25. "Odd that the homeless children, the silt of war frenzy, could initiate me into the brotherhood of man."

26. "My tears were not for Bailey or Mother or even myself but for the helplessness of mortals who live on the sufferance of Life. In order to avoid this bitter end, we would all have to be born again, and born with the knowledge of alternatives."

27. "Without knowing it, I had gone from being ignorant of being ignorant to being aware of being aware."

28. "To be left alone on the tight rope of youthful knowing is to experience the excruciating beauty of full freedom and the threat of eternal indecision."

LESSON FOURTEEN

Objective
>   To review all of the vocabulary work done in this unit

VOCABULARY REVIEW ACTIVITIES

1. Divide your class into two teams and have an old-fashioned spelling or definition bee.

2. Give each of your students (or students in groups of two, three or four) an *I Know Why the Caged Bird Sings* Vocabulary Word Search Puzzle. The person (group) to find all of the vocabulary words in the puzzle first wins.

3. Give students an *I Know Why the Caged Bird Sings* Vocabulary Word Search Puzzle without the word list. The person or group to find the most vocabulary words in the puzzle wins.

4. Use an *I Know Why the Caged Bird Sings* Vocabulary Crossword Puzzle. Put the puzzle onto a transparency on the overhead projector (so everyone can see it), and do the puzzle together as a class.

5. Give students an *I Know Why the Caged Bird Sings* Vocabulary Matching Worksheet to do.

6. Divide your class into two teams. Use the *I Know Why the Caged Bird Sings* vocabulary words with their letters jumbled as a word list. Student 1 from Team A faces off against Student 1 from Team B. You write the first jumbled word on the board. The first student (1A or 1B) to unscramble the word wins the chance for his/her team to score points. If 1A wins the jumble, go to student 2A and give him/her a definition. He/she must give you the correct spelling of the vocabulary word which fits that definition. If he/she does, Team A scores a point, and you give student 3A a definition for which you expect a correctly spelled matching vocabulary word. Continue giving Team A definitions until some team member makes an incorrect response. An incorrect response sends the game back to the jumbled-word face off, this time with students 2A and 2B. Instead of repeating giving definitions to the first few students of each team, continue with the student after the one who gave the last incorrect response on the team. For example, if Team B wins the jumbled-word face-off, and student 5B gave the last incorrect answer for Team B, you would start this round of definition questions with student 6B, and so on. The team with the most points wins!

7. Have students write a story in which they correctly use as many vocabulary words as possible. Have students read their compositions orally. Post the most original compositions on your bulletin board!

LESSON FIFTEEN

Objective
1. To give the students the opportunity to practice writing to persuade
2. To give the teacher the opportunity to evaluate the students' writing skills

Activity

Distribute Writing Assignment #3. Discuss the directions in detail and give students ample time to complete the assignment.

LESSON SIXTEEN

Objectives
1. To watch the movie version of *I Know Why the Caged Bird Sings*.
2. To compare and contrast the movie and the book

Activity #1

Watch the movie version of *I Know Why the Caged Bird Sings*.

Activity #2

Compare and contrast the movie and the book. Discuss the changes, and the possible reasons for them.

LESSON SEVENTEEN

Objectives
1. To widen the breadth of students' knowledge about the topics discussed or touched upon in *I Know Why the Caged Bird Sings*
2. To check students' non-fiction assignments

Activity

Ask each student to give a brief oral report about the nonfiction work he/she read for the nonfiction assignment. Your criteria for evaluating this report will vary depending on the level of your students. You may wish for students to give a complete report without using notes of any kind, or you may want students to read directly from a written report, or you may want to do something in between these two extremes. Just make students aware of your criteria in ample time for them to prepare their reports.

Start with one student's report, After that, ask if anyone else in the class has read on a topic related to the first student's report. If no one has, choose another student at random. After each report, be sure to ask if anyone has a report related to the one just completed. That will help keep a continuity during the discussion of the reports.

WRITING ASSIGNMENT # 3   *I Know Why the Caged Bird Sings.*

PROMPT

You have completed your resume (Writing Assignment #2.) You have been notified that you will be interviewed next week. Just as Maya Angelou was the first Black person to work on the cable cars in San Francisco, you will be the first person of your gender or ethnic background to hold this job. In the interview, you need to persuade the employer that you are the best person for the job. One way to prepare for an interview is to write all of your thoughts down on paper first.

PREWRITING

Make sure you know what the employer's needs are, who his/her clients are, and what the business or service provided is like. Then decide what kind of things the employer needs to know about you, and how you would be an asset to the company. Think of every possible reason the person might hesitate to hire you, and think of a counter-argument stating why he/she should hire you. Make sure to include an argument in favor of including someone of your gender or ethnic background in his/her workforce.

DRAFTING

Write out the list of possible interview questions and your answers. You may need to revise this several times before you get the wording to be as effective as possible. Make sure you are using strong verbs and adjectives to describe yourself. It can help to read your draft aloud, and listen to see if your words sound sincere and convincing.

PROMPT

When you finish the rough draft, ask another student to look at it. You may even want to read it aloud for the student. After reading/listening, he/she should tell you what he/she liked best about your paper, which parts were difficult to understand or needed more information, and ways in which your work could be improved. Reread your paper considering your critic's comments, and make the corrections you think are necessary.

PROOFREADING

Do a final proofreading of your paper, double-checking your grammar, spelling, organization, and the clarity of your ideas.

LESSON EIGHTEEN

Objective
To review the main ideas presented in *I Know Why the Caged Bird Sings*

Activity #1
Choose one of the review games/activities included in the packet and spend your class period as outlined there.

Activity #2
Remind students of the date for the Unit Test. Stress the review of the Study Guides and their class notes as a last minute, brush-up review for homework.

REVIEW GAMES / ACTIVITIES

1. Ask the class to make up a unit test for *I Know Why the Caged Bird Sings*. The test should have 4 sections: multiple choice, true/false, short answer and essay. Students may use 1/2 period to make the test, including a separate answer sheet, and then swap papers and use the other 1/2 class period to take a test a classmate has devised. (open book)

2. Take 1/2 period for students to make up true and false questions (including the answers). Collect the papers and divide the class into two teams. Draw a big tic-tac-toe board on the chalk board. Make one team X and one team O. Ask questions to each side, giving each student one turn. If the question is answered correctly, that student's team's letter (X or O) is placed in the box. If the answer is incorrect, no mark is placed in the box. The object is to get three marks in a row like tic-tac-toe. You may want to keep track of the number of games won for each team.

3. Take 1/2 period for students to make up questions (true/false and short answer). Collect the questions. Divide the class into two teams. You'll alternate asking questions to individual members of teams A & B (like in a spelling bee). The question keeps going from A to B until it is correctly answered, then a new question is asked. A correct answer does not allow the team to get another question. Correct answers are +2 points; incorrect answers are -1 point.

4. Allow students time to quiz each other (in pairs) from their study guides and class notes.

5. Give students a *I Know Why the Caged Bird Sings* crossword puzzle to complete.

6. Divide your class into two teams. Use the *I Know Why the Caged Bird Sings* crossword words with their letters jumbled as a word list. Student 1 from Team A faces off against Student 1 from Team B. You write the first jumbled word on the board. The first student (1A or 1B) to unscramble the word wins the chance for his/her team to score points. If 1A wins the jumble, go to student 2A and give him/her a clue. He/she must give you the correct word which matches that clue. If he/she does, Team A scores a point, and you give student 3A a clue for which you expect another correct response. Continue giving Team A clues until some team member makes an incorrect response. An incorrect response sends the game back to the jumbled-word face off, this time with students 2A and 2B. Instead of repeating giving clues to the first few students of each team, continue with the student after the one who gave the last incorrect response on the team.

7. Take on the persona of "The Answer Person." Allow students to ask any question about the book. Answer the questions, or tell students where to look in the book to find the answer.

8. Students may enjoy playing charades with events from the story. Select a student to start. Give him/her a card with a scene or event from the story. Allow the players to use their books to find the scene being described. The first person to guess each charade performs the next one.

9. Play a categories-type quiz game. (A master is included in this Unit Plan). Make an overhead transparency of the categories form. Divide the class into teams of three or four players each. Have each team choose a recorder and a banker. choose a team to go first. That team will choose a category and point amount. Ask the question to the entire class.(Use the Study Guide Quiz and Vocabulary questions.) Give the teams one minute to discuss the answer and write it down. Walk around the room and check the answers. Each team that answers correctly receives the points. (Incorrect answers are not penalized; they just don't receive any points). Cross out that square on the playing board. Play continues until all squares have been used. The winning team is the one with the most points. You can assign bonus points to any square or squares you choose.

10. Have students complete the last column (What I Learned) of the KWL sheet you distributed in Lesson One. Discuss their answers with the class.

NOTE: If students do not need the extra review, omit this lesson and go on to the test.

QUIZ GAME
I Know Why the Caged Bird Sings

Vocabulary	Chapters 1-12	Chapters 13-21	Chapters 21-29	Chapters 30-36
100	100	100	100	100
200	200	200	200	200
300	300	300	300	300
400	400	400	400	400
500	500	500	500	500

UNIT TESTS

SHORT ANSWER UNIT TEST #1 - *I Know Why the Caged Bird Sings*

I. Matching/Identify

____ 1. Maya   A. fought with Marguerite and cut her
____ 2. Marguerite   B. crippled as a child
____ 3. Momma   C. nickname given to the author by her brother
____ 4. Bailey   D. often traveled to Mexico
____ 5. Vivian Baxter   E. Marguerite's first real girlfriend
____ 6. Uncle Willie   F. author's real name
____ 7. Mrs. Flowers   G. Marguerite's mother
____ 8. Dolores   H. owner of the Store in Stamps, Arkansas
____ 9. Louise Kendricks   I. gave Marguerite the gift of books
____ 10. Daddy Bailey   J. beloved brother of Marguerite

II. Short Answer

1. With whom did Marguerite and Bailey live at the beginning of the book?

2. What, according to the author, was the one thing about the whites that was most enviable?

3. What happened to Marguerite as a result of the experience with Mr. Freeman?

Caged Bird Short Answer Unit Test 1 Page 2

4. What is the author's theory about divine intervention?

5. What was Marguerite's reaction to the graduation speech?

6. What was the enigma of which Maya Angelou spoke?

7. How did Bailey and Marguerite learn there were other people in the world?

Caged Bird Short Answer Unit Test 1 Page 3

8. Who, according to the author, is the hero of the Black ghetto?

9. What insight did Marguerite have into her father's personality on their trip to Mexico?

10. According to the author, what forces assault the young Black female?

Caged Bird Short Answer Unit Test 1 Page 4

III. Essay

    Give your impression of Maya Angelou. Explain in detail using examples from her autobiography.

Caged Bird Short Answer Unit Test 1 Page 5

IV. Vocabulary

Listen to the vocabulary words and spell them. After you have spelled all the words, go back and write down the definitions.

KEY: SHORT ANSWER UNIT TEST 1 - *Caged Bird*

I. Matching/Identify

C	1. Maya	A.	fought with Marguerite and cut her
F	2. Marguerite	B.	crippled as a child
H	3. Momma	C.	nickname given to the author by her brother
J	4. Bailey	D.	often traveled to Mexico
G	5. Vivian Baxter	E.	Marguerite's first real girlfriend
B	6. Uncle Willie	F.	author's real name
I	7. Mrs. Flowers	G.	Marguerite's mother
A	8. Dolores	H.	owner of the Store in Stamps, Arkansas
E	9. Louise Kendricks	I.	gave Marguerite the gift of books
D	10. Daddy Bailey	J.	beloved brother of Marguerite

II. Short Answer

1. With whom did Marguerite and Bailey live at the beginning of the book?
   They lived with their father's mother in Stamps, Arkansas.

2. What, according to the author, was the one thing about the whites that was most enviable?
   It was their wealth that allowed them to waste.

3. What happened to Marguerite as a result of the experience with Mr. Freeman?
   She stopped talking to everyone except Bailey. She thought that if she talked to anyone, that person might die, too.

4. What is the author's theory about divine intervention?
   The author believes that poor people attribute their existence and future to divine intervention. As people become more affluent, God descends in responsibility for their lives.

5. What was Marguerite's reaction to the graduation speech?
   The graduation speech made Marguerite angry and sick at heart. He was assuming that the Black student would become athletes, farmer, maids, or have other lowly jobs, while the white students would go on to college and whatever professions they chose.

6. What was the enigma of which Maya Angelou spoke?

It was the "humorless puzzle of inequality and hate."

7. How did Bailey and Marguerite learn there were other people in the world?
   They learned it through food. Their mother took them to many ethnic restaurants.

8. Who, according to the author, is the hero of the Black ghetto?
   "... the hero is that man who is offered only the crumbs from his country's table but by ingenuity and courage is able to take for himself a Lucullan feast."

9. What insight did Marguerite have into her father's personality on their trip to Mexico?
   She realized that he must have been frustrated living in Stamps. He had aspirations of grandeur. She also discovered that under his facade, he was lonely and constantly searching for his place in the world.

10. According to the author, what forces assault the young Black female?
    The young Black female is assaulted by the common forces of nature, masculine prejudice, white illogical hate, and Black lack of power.

III. Essay   Grade these on your own criteria.

IV. Vocabulary Choose ten of the vocabulary words to read orally to your class for this part of the test.

SHORT ANSWER UNIT TEST 2 - *Caged Bird*

I. Matching

____ 1. Maya   A. Marguerite's first real girlfriend
____ 2. Marguerite   B. gave Marguerite the gift of books
____ 3. Momma   C. Marguerite's mother
____ 4. Bailey   D. owner of the Store in Stamps, Arkansas
____ 5. Vivian Baxter   E. nickname given to the author by her brother
____ 6. Uncle Willie   F. often traveled to Mexico
____ 7. Mrs. Flowers   G. fought with Marguerite and cut her
____ 8. Dolores   H. crippled as a child
____ 9. Louise Kendricks I. beloved brother of Marguerite
____ 10. Daddy Bailey   J. author's real name

II. Short Answer

1. According to the author, what forces assault the young Black female?

2. What, according to the author, was the one thing about the whites that was most enviable?

3. What insight did Marguerite have into her father's personality on their trip to Mexico?

Caged Bird Short Answer Unit Test 2 Page 2

4. Who according to the author, is the hero of the Black ghetto?

5. How did Bailey and Marguerite learn there were other people in the world?

6. What was the enigma of which Maya Angelou spoke?

7. What was Marguerite's reaction to the graduation speech?

Caged Bird Short Answer Unit Test 2 Page 3

8. What is the author's theory about divine intervention?

9. What happened to Marguerite as a result of the experience with Mr. Freeman?

10. With whom did Marguerite and Bailey live at the beginning of the book?

Caged Bird Short Answer Unit Test 2 Page 4

III. Essay

What insights into the life of the American rural African-American community does the author provide in this book?

Caged Bird Short Answer Unit Test 2 Page 5

IV. Vocabulary

Listen to the vocabulary words and spell them. After you have spelled all the words, go back and write down the definitions.

ANSWER KEY SHORT ANSWER UNIT TEST 2 - *Caged Bird*

Use this key for the matching test for Short Answer Test 2 and the Advanced Short Answer Test.

I. Matching

E	1.	Maya	A.	Marguerite's first real girlfriend
J	2.	Marguerite	B.	gave Marguerite the gift of books
D	3.	Momma	C.	Marguerite's mother
I	4.	Bailey	D.	owner of the Store in Stamps, Arkansas
C	5.	Vivian Baxter	E.	nickname given to the author by her brother
H	6.	Uncle Willie	F.	often traveled to Mexico
B	7.	Mrs. Flowers	G.	fought with Marguerite and cut her
G	8.	Dolores	H.	crippled as a child
A	9.	Louise Kendricks	I.	beloved brother of Marguerite
F	10.	Daddy Bailey	J.	author's real name

II. Short Answer

1. According to the author, what forces assault the young Black female?
    The young Black female is assaulted by the common forces of nature, masculine prejudice, white illogical hate, and Black lack of power.

2. What, according to the author, was the one thing about the whites that was most enviable?
    It was their wealth that allowed them to waste.

3. What insight did Marguerite have into her father's personality on their trip to Mexico?
    She realized that he must have been frustrated living in Stamps. He had aspirations of grandeur. She also discovered that under his facade, he was lonely and constantly searching for his place in the world.

4. Who, according to the author, is the hero of the Black ghetto?
    ". . . the hero is that man who is offered only the crumbs from his country's table but by ingenuity and courage is able to take for himself a Lucullan feast."

5. How did Bailey and Marguerite learn there were other people in the world?
    They learned it through food. Their mother took them to many ethnic restaurants.

6. What was the enigma of which Maya Angelou spoke?
    It was the "humorless puzzle of inequality and hate."

7. What was Marguerite's reaction to the graduation speech?
    The graduation speech made Marguerite angry and sick at heart.

8. What is the author's theory about divine intervention?
    The author believes that poor people attribute their existence and future to divine intervention. As people become more affluent, God descends in responsibility for their lives.

9. What happened to Marguerite as a result of the experience with Mr. Freeman?
    She stopped talking to everyone except Bailey. She thought that if she talked to anyone, that person might die, too.

10. With whom did Marguerite and Bailey live at the beginning of the book?
    They lived with their father's mother in Stamps, Arkansas.

III. Essay   Grade the essay on your own criteria

IV. Vocabulary Choose ten of the vocabulary words to read orally to your students for this section of the test.

ADVANCED SHORT ANSWER TEST - *Caged Bird*

I. Matching

_____ 1. Maya A. Marguerite's first real girlfriend
_____ 2. Marguerite B. gave Marguerite the gift of books
_____ 3. Momma C. Marguerite's mother
_____ 4. Bailey D. owner of the Store in Stamps, Arkansas
_____ 5. Vivian Baxter E. nickname given to the author by her brother
_____ 6. Uncle Willie F. often traveled to Mexico
_____ 7. Mrs. Flowers G. fought with Marguerite and cut her
_____ 8. Dolores H. crippled as a child
_____ 9. Louise Kendricks I. beloved brother of Marguerite
_____ 10. Daddy Bailey J. author's real name

II. Short Answer

1. From what point of view is the book written? How does this affect your understanding of the story?

2. Which events in the book seemed to have been the most positive influences on Ms. Angelou?

Caged Bird Advanced Short Answer Unit Test Page 2

3. Discuss the role of imagery in *I Know Why the Caged Bird Sings*.

4. What do you think Maya Angelou learned from each of the important people in her life?

5. Which of the personalities (other than Ms. Angelou) in the book seemed to be the most fully developed?

Caged Bird Advanced Short Answer Unit Test Page 3

III. Quotations

Explain the importance and meaning of the following quotations.

1. "Because I was really white and because a cruel fairy stepmother , who was understandably jealous of my beauty, had turned me into a too-big Negro girl, with nappy black hair, broad feet and a space between her teeth that would hold a number two pencil."

2. "But it was Shakespeare who said, 'When in disgrace with fortune and men's eyes.' It was a state with which I felt myself most familiar. I pacified myself about his whiteness by saying that after all he had been dead so long it couldn't matter to anyone anymore."

3. "I was liked, and what a difference it made. I was respected not as Mrs. Henderson's grandchild or Bailey's sister but just for being Marguerite Johnson."

Caged Bird Advanced Short Answer Unit Test Page 4

4. "It was awful to be Negro and have no control over my life. It was brutal to be young and already trained to sit quietly and listen to charges brought against my color with no chance of defense."

5. "Mother whispered, 'See, you don't have to think about doing the right thing. If you're for the right thing, then you do it without thinking.' "

Caged Bird Advanced Short Answer Unit Test Page 5

IV. Vocabulary

      Listen to the vocabulary words and write them down. After you have written down all of the words, write a paragraph in which you use all the words. The paragraph must in some way relate to *I Know Why the Caged Bird Sings*.

MULTIPLE CHOICE UNIT TEST 1 - *Caged Bird*

I. Matching/Identify

1. Maya
2. Marguerite
3. Momma
4. Bailey
5. Vivian Baxter
6. Uncle Willie
7. Mrs. Flowers
8. Dolores
9. Louise Kendricks
10. Daddy Bailey

A. fought with Marguerite and cut her
B. crippled as a child
C. nickname given to the author by her brother
D. often traveled to Mexico
E. Marguerite's first real girlfriend
F. author's real name
G. Marguerite's mother
H. owner of the Store in Stamps, Arkansas
I. gave Marguerite the gift of books
J. beloved brother of Marguerite

II. Multiple Choice

1. With whom did Marguerite and Bailey live at the beginning of the book?
    A. They lived with an aunt in Los Angeles.
    B. They lived with their older sister in St. Louis.
    C. They lived in a foster home in San Francisco.
    D. They lived with their father's mother in Stamps, Arkansas.

2. What, according to the author, was the one thing about the whites that was most enviable?
    A. It was their white skin.
    B. It was their self-confidence.
    C. It was their wealth that allowed them to waste.
    D. It was the fact that they could go anywhere they pleased.

3. What happened to Marguerite as a result of the experience with Mr. Freeman?
    A. She stopped talking to everyone except Bailey. She thought that if she talked to anyone, that person might die, too.
    B. She got very wild, and started taking dangerous risks.
    C. She locked herself in a dark room and refused to come out.
    D. She screamed every time a man came near her.

Caged Bird Multiple Choice Test 1 Page 2

4. True or False: The author believes that poor people attribute their existence and future to divine intervention. As people become more affluent, God descends in responsibility for their lives.
    A. True
    B. False

5. True or False: The graduation speech made Marguerite angry and sick at heart.
    A. True
    B. False

6. What was the enigma of which Maya Angelou spoke?
    A. It was good vs. evil.
    B. It was suffering on Earth to receive a reward in Heaven.
    C. It was inequality and hate.
    D. It was determining which course of action was really the correct one.

7. How did Bailey and Marguerite learn there were other people in the world?
    A. They were in a multi-racial high school.
    B. They watched a lot of television.
    C. They learned it through food. Their mother took them to many ethnic restaurants.
    D. They read a lot of books and magazines.

8. Who is the author describing? ". . . that man who is offered only the crumbs from his country's table but by ingenuity and courage is able to take for himself a Lucullan feast."
    A. She is describing the black businessman.
    B. She is describing the hero of the Black ghetto.
    C. She is describing share-croppers in the South.
    D. She is describing the main character in a novel she was writing

9. True or False: On their trip to Mexico, Marguerite discovered that under his facade, her father was lonely and constantly searching for his place in the world.
    A. True
    B. False

10. Which of the following forces did **not** assault the young Black female?
    A. the common forces of nature
    B. masculine prejudice
    C. white illogical hate
    D. jealousy

Caged Bird Multiple Choice Test 1 Page 2

III. Vocabulary Matching

1. taffeta
2. paranoia
3. rancor
4. pandemonium
5. droll
6. deftness
7. quandary
8. mote
9. frivolity
10. blasphemous
11. expeditious
12. mollified
13. excruciating
14. retributive
15. dissipate
16. recriminations
17. pretense
18. deferential
19. ostensibly
20. malaise

A. quickness, skillfulness
B. calmed, soothed
C. appearing as such
D. silliness
E. a crisp fabric with a slight sheen
F. demanded in payment
G. a state of uncertainty or perplexity
H. extreme, irrational distrust of others
I. countercharges
J. speaking irreverently about a sacred being
K. a general sense of depression
L. courteous, respectful
M. intensely painful
N. false appearance
O. a speck
P. bitter, long-lasting resentment
Q. done with speed and efficiency
R. amusingly odd
S. to drive away; disperse
T. wild uproar or noise

MULTIPLE CHOICE UNIT TEST 2 - *Caged Bird*

I. Matching

1. Maya
2. Marguerite
3. Momma
4. Bailey
5. Vivian Baxter
6. Uncle Willie
7. Mrs. Flowers
8. Dolores
9. Louise Kendricks
10. Daddy Bailey

A. Marguerite's first real girlfriend
B. gave Marguerite the gift of books
C. Marguerite's mother
D. owner of the Store in Stamps, Arkansas
E. nickname given to the author by her brother
F. often traveled to Mexico
G. fought with Marguerite and cut her
H. crippled as a child
I. beloved brother of Marguerite
J. author's real name

II. Multiple Choice

1. Which of the following forces did **not** assault the young Black female?
    A. the common forces of nature
    B. masculine prejudice
    C. white illogical hate
    D. jealousy

2. True or False: The graduation speech made Marguerite angry and sick at heart.
    A. True
    B. False

3. With whom did Marguerite and Bailey live at the beginning of the book?
    A. They lived with an aunt in Los Angeles.
    B. They lived with their older sister in St. Louis.
    C. They lived in a foster home in San Francisco.
    D. They lived with their father's mother in Stamps, Arkansas.

4. True or False: On their trip to Mexico, Marguerite discovered that under his facade, her father was lonely and constantly searching for his place in the world.
    A. True
    B. False

Caged Bird Multiple Choice Test 2 Page 2

5. True or False: The author believes that poor people attribute their existence and future to divine intervention. As people become more affluent, God descends in responsibility for their lives.
   A. True
   B. False

6. What, according to the author, was the one thing about the whites that was most enviable?
   A. It was their white skin.
   B. It was their self-confidence.
   C. It was their wealth that allowed them to waste.
   D. It was the fact that they could go anywhere they pleased.

7. Who is the author describing? "... that man who is offered only the crumbs from his country's table but by ingenuity and courage is able to take for himself a Lucullan feast."
   A. She is describing the black businessman.
   B. She is describing the hero of the Black ghetto.
   C. She is describing share-croppers in the South.
   D. She is describing the main character in a novel she was writing

8. What was the enigma of which Maya Angelou spoke?
   A. It was good vs. evil.
   B. It was suffering on Earth to receive a reward in Heaven.
   C. It was inequality and hate.
   D. It was determining which course of action was really the correct one.

9. What happened to Marguerite as a result of the experience with Mr. Freeman?
   A. She stopped talking to everyone except Bailey. She thought that if she talked to anyone, that person might die, too.
   B. She got very wild, and started taking dangerous risks.
   C. She locked herself in a dark room and refused to come out.
   D. She screamed every time a man came near her.

10. How did Bailey and Marguerite learn there were other people in the world?
    A. They were in a multi-racial high school.
    B. They watched a lot of television.
    C. They learned it through food. Their mother took them to many ethnic restaurants.
    D. They read a lot of books and magazines.

Caged Bird Multiple Choice Test 2 Page 3

III. Vocabulary (Matching)

1.	sparse	A.	excluded or banished from a group
2.	appellations	B.	highly elaborate, showy
3.	flamboyant	C.	restricted; restrained
4.	admonished	D.	impulsiveness
5.	infuse	E.	rough-sounding
6.	inscrutable	F.	jarring, discordant sound
7.	commensurate	G.	to fill with something
8.	raucous	H.	rosy colored
9.	ecumenical	I.	brief statements of principles
10.	trammeled	J.	refuting
11.	rebutting	K.	gently reproved
12.	enigma	L.	promoting unity among religions
13.	florid	M.	names, titles, or designations
14.	cajoled	N.	of the same size or proportion
15.	cacophony	O.	urged gently
16.	approbation	P.	showing haughty disdain
17.	supercilious	Q.	difficult to understand
18.	aphorisms	R.	an expression of warm approval; praise
19.	ostracized	S.	something puzzling or inexplicable
20.	capriciousness	T.	occurring at widely spaced intervals

ANSWER SHEET
Multiple Choice Unit Tests

I. Matching

1. _____
2. _____
3. _____
4. _____
5. _____
6. _____
7. _____
8. _____
9. _____
10. _____

II. Multiple Choice

1. (A) (B) (C) (D)
2. (A) (B) (C) (D)
3. (A) (B) (C) (D)
4. (A) (B) (C) (D)
5. (A) (B) (C) (D)
6. (A) (B) (C) (D)
7. (A) (B) (C) (D)
8. (A) (B) (C) (D)
9. (A) (B) (C) (D)
10. (A) (B) (C) (D)

III. Vocabulary

1. _____
2. _____
3. _____
4. _____
5. _____
6. _____
7. _____
8. _____
9. _____
10. _____
11. _____
12. _____
13. _____
14. _____
15. _____
16. _____
17. _____
18. _____
19. _____
20. _____

ANSWER SHEET KEY *I Know Why the Caged Bird Sings*
Multiple Choice Unit Test 1

I. Matching

1. C
2. F
3. H
4. J
5. G
6. B
7. I
8. A
9. E
10. D

II. Multiple Choice

1. (A) (B) (C) ( )
2. (A) (B) ( ) (D)
3. ( ) (B) (C) (D)
4. ( ) (B) (C) (D)
5. ( ) (B) (C) (D)
6. (A) (B) ( ) (D)
7. (A) (B) ( ) (D)
8. (A) ( ) (C) (D)
9. ( ) (B) (C) (D)
10. (A) (B) (C) ( )

III. Vocabulary

1. E
2. H
3. P
4. T
5. R
6. A
7. G
8. O
9. D
10. J
11. Q
12. B
13. M
14. F
15. S
16. I
17. N
18. L
19. C
20. K

ANSWER SHEET KEY *I Know Why the Caged Bird Sings*
Multiple Choice Unit Test 2

I. Matching

1. E
2. J
3. D
4. I
5. C
6. H
7. B
8. G
9. A
10. F

II. Multiple Choice

1. (A) (B) (C) ( )
2. ( ) (B) (C) (D)
3. (A) (B) (C) ( )
4. ( ) (B) (C) (D)
5. ( ) (B) (C) (D)
6. (A) (B) ( ) (D)
7. (A) ( ) (C) (D)
8. (A) (B) ( ) (D)
9. ( ) (B) (C) (D)
10. (A) (B) ( ) (D)

IV. Vocabulary

1. T
2. M
3. B
4. K
5. G
6. Q
7. N
8. E
9. L
10. C
11. J
12. S
13. H
14. O
15. F
16. R
17. P
18. I
19. A
20. D

UNIT RESOURCE MATERIALS

BULLETIN BOARD IDEAS - *I Know Why The Caged Bird Sings*

1. Save one corner of the board for the best of students' *Caged Bird* writing assignments. You may want to use background maps of Arkansas, Missouri, and California to represent the places where Maya Angelou lived.

2. Take one of the word search puzzles from the extra activities packet and with a marker copy it over in a large size on the bulletin board. Write the clue words to find to one side. Invite students prior to and after class to find the words and circle them on the bulletin board.

3. Have students find or draw pictures they think resemble the people in the book.

4. Invite students to help make an interactive bulletin board quiz. Give each student a half sheet of paper folded in half so it can open like a little book. On the outside flap, have each student write a description of one of the characters in the text. On the inside, they will write the name of the character. You can staple or tack these papers to the bulletin board so students can read the descriptions and lift the flaps to find the answers.

5. Collect pictures of the cities mentioned in the book.

6. Make a display of pictures or book jackets representing all of Maya Angelou's works.

7. Make a display of travel posters of Arkansas, California, and Missouri.

8. Display articles about Maya Angelou and critiques of her works.

9. Have students design postcards depicting scenes in the book and use those for your bulletin board.

10. Do a compar/contrast display. On one side of the board, display pictures and writings that deal with life in a rural area. On the other side, display pictures and writings that deal with life in an urban area.

EXTRA ACTIVITIES - *I Know Why the Caged Bird Sings*

One of the difficulties in teaching a novel is that all students don't read at the same speed. One student who likes to read may take the book home and finish it in a day or two. Sometimes a few students finish the in-class assignments early. The problem, then, is finding suitable extra activities for students.

One thing that helps is to keep a little library of books and magazines related to the novel in the classroom. For this unit, you might check out other books by Maya Angelou. A biography of the author would be interesting for some students. There are also many books by other African-American authors students might enjoy reading. Several journals have critiques of Maya Angelou's works. Some of the students may enjoy reading these and responding either in writing or in discussion groups.

Other things you may keep on hand are puzzles and worksheets. Several of these relating to *Caged Bird* are included in this unit. Feel free to duplicate them for your class.

Some students may like to draw. You might devise a contest or allow some extra-credit grade for students who draw characters or scenes from this novel. Note, too, that if the students do not want to keep their drawings, you may pick up some extra bulletin board materials this way. If you have a contest and supply a prize, you could, possible make the drawing itself a non-refundable entry fee.

Have maps, a globe, and travel brochures on hand for easy reference. Travel agencies and automobile clubs are good sources for these materials.

The pages which follow contain games, puzzles and worksheets. There are two main groups of activities: one group for the unit words (that is, words generally relating to the content of the text) and another group of activities for the vocabulary words.

The object here is to provide you with some extra materials you may use in any way you choose.

MORE ACTIVITIES - *I Know Why The Caged Bird Sings*

1. Pick one of the incidents for students to dramatize. Encourage students to write dialog for the characters. Perhaps you could assign various stories to different groups of students so more than one story could be acted and more students could participate.

2. Have students design a book cover (front and back and inside flaps) for *I Know Why The Caged Bird Sings*.

3. Have students design a bulletin board (ready to be put up–not just sketched) for *Caged Bird*.

4. Invite a story teller to tell one or more stories related to *Caged Bird*.

5. Have students create a *Caged Bird* newspaper. Assign teams of students to write news articles based on the events from the book. An editorial team could review the articles and a production team could publish the newspaper.

6. Help students design and produce a talk show. Choose one of the story incidents as the topic. The host will interview the various characters. Students should make up the questions they want the host to ask the characters.

7. Invite students who have read other books by Maya Angelou to present book talks to the class.

8. Students may enjoy reading some of Ms. Angelou's poetry to the class.

9. Several of Maya Angelou's books and poetry collections are available on audio tape. Play some of these for the class. Her inaugural address poem for President Clinton may be of special interest.

10. Research the effects of World War II on the work force and the economy of the United States to understand the changes she talked about in Chapters 26 through 36.

11. Create other titles for the book.

12. Invite someone who has lived in one of the areas mentioned in the book to speak to the class.

I Know Why The Caged Bird Sings Word Search

```
H P R E G N A N C Y S T A M P S W T E
E E W E A L T H X R H C F O O Z C S F
R Y N J S S S L D A A U L M P N I G Q
O V W D F B A R T M K L O M B U R N Y
S X I F E Y C Y R D E L W A O O R O C
E Y L F O R X W A O S L E L J L Z S E
G C L L F B S D S N P I R K U E W V E
R D I L L A Z O H L E N S M N G Q I L
E R E R V I G F N E A A T R K N M V R
G N N G E L E S L A R N Z W Y A T I L
A O C I X E M F Z V E V V D A P Z A R
T G N D M Y P F R Y K V R O R L Z N T
I I J N W M M R P A Z J N L D G Y E N
O G F W Z O B E R B N P J O S J E E Z
N G C G D L K E Z L G C X R K R G C P
N L N G H S Z M S O N M I E T P S Y D
A E N X Q T R A I N S M R S S I U O L
L I N C O L N Z D M B J P C X G J Y
K I R W I N C K R E Z T A Y L O R Y Q
```

ANGELES	GIGGLE	LOUIS	SEGREGATION
ANGELOU	GOD	LOUISE	SHAKESPEARE
BAILEY	HENDERSON	LOYAL	STAMPS
BLONDE	HERO	MARY	STREET
CULLLINAN	JOYCE	MEXICO	TAYLOR
DOLORES	JUNKYARD	MOMMA	TRAIN
DONLEAVY	KINGDOM	MONROE	TRASH
FLOWERS	KIRWIN	MRS	VIVIAN
FRANCISCO	KLAN	PREGNANCY	WEALTH
FREEMAN	LINCOLN	PURSE	WILLIE

I Know Why The Caged Bird Sings Word Search Answer Key

```
H  P  R  E  G  N  A  N  C  Y  S  T  A  M  P  S        E
E  E  W  E  A  L  T  H     R  H  C  F  O  O     S
R     N           L        A  U  L  M  P  N  I
O     W  D        A     T  M  K  O  M     U  R
S     I     E           R  D  E  L  W  O  O  R  O
E     L     O  R        A  O  S  L  E  L  J  L     S  E
G     L  L  B  S        S  N  P  I  R  U  E  V     E
R     I     A     O     H  L  E  N  S  N  G  I
E     E     I     N     E  A  A     K  N  V
G  A  N  G  E  L  E  S     A  R  N     Y  A  I
A  O  C  I  X  E  M  F     V  E        D  A  A
T  G           Y     F  R  Y           O  R  N  T
I  I           M  R  E  A              L  D  E
O  G        O     E  B  N     C        O     E  E
N  G     D        E  L     C           R  R  C
N  L  G           M  O        I     T     Y  D
A  E        T  R  A  I  N     M  R  S  S  I  U  O
L  I  N  C  O  L  N  N        D           C  G  J  L
K  I  R  W  I  N           E     T  A  Y  L  O  R
```

ANGELES	GIGGLE	LOUIS	SEGREGATION
ANGELOU	GOD	LOUISE	SHAKESPEARE
BAILEY	HENDERSON	LOYAL	STAMPS
BLONDE	HERO	MARY	STREET
CULLLINAN	JOYCE	MEXICO	TAYLOR
DOLORES	JUNKYARD	MOMMA	TRAIN
DONLEAVY	KINGDOM	MONROE	TRASH
FLOWERS	KIRWIN	MRS	VIVIAN
FRANCISCO	KLAN	PREGNANCY	WEALTH
FREEMAN	LINCOLN	PURSE	WILLIE

CROSSWORD I Know Why The Caged Bird Sings

Across
1. Uncle ___ was crippled as a child
4. Los ___; Daddy Bailey's home
6. Marguerite's new name
7. Teacher in love with information & treated students respectfully
8. Johnson children's method of travel to Stamps
9. Searched for a Black man
11. Sister ___ got carried away at church services
12. Marguerite lived here for one month
15. Attribute of Baxter clan
17. Mother Dear; ___ Baxter
19. This title for Momma in court proved her worth and dignity
20. Owner of the store
21. Marguerite was first Negro to work on the ____ cars

Down
1. Enviable attribute of whites
2. Marguerite dreamed she would one day have __ hair and blue eyes
3. Powhite___ mocked and insulted Momma
4. Maya ___; author
5. According to Marguerite, he was white but not prejudiced
7. Marguerite described Bailey as her ___ Come
10. Mr. ____ sexually abused Marguerite
11. Marguerite drove home from this place
12. Bailey's first love
13. Mrs. ____ gave Marguerite the gift of books
14. What Louise taught Marguerite to do
16. Dr. ___ wouldn't treat Marguerite's tooth
18. City in Arkansas where author lived

CROSSWORD ANSWER KEY I Know Why The Caged Bird Sings

Across
1. Uncle ___ was crippled as a child
4. Los ___; Daddy Bailey's home
6. Marguerite's new name
7. Teacher in love with information & treated students respectfully
8. Johnson children's method of travel to Stamps
9. Searched for a Black man
11. Sister ___ got carried away at church services
12. Marguerite lived here for one month
15. Attribute of Baxter clan
17. Mother Dear; ___ Baxter
19. This title for Momma in court proved her worth and dignity
20. Owner of the store
21. Marguerite was first Negro to work on the ____ cars

Down
1. Enviable attribute of whites
2. Marguerite dreamed she would one day have __ hair and blue eyes
3. Powhite___ mocked and insulted Momma
4. Maya ___; author
5. According to Marguerite, he was white but not prejudiced
7. Marguerite described Bailey as her ___ Come
10. Mr. ____ sexually abused Marguerite
11. Marguerite drove home from this place
12. Bailey's first love
13. Mrs. ____ gave Marguerite the gift of books
14. What Louise taught Marguerite to do
16. Dr. ___ wouldn't treat Marguerite's tooth
18. City in Arkansas where author lived

MATCHING WORKSHEET 1 - *I Know Why The Caged Bird Sings*

_____ 1. MAYA ANGELOU   A. Crippled as a child
_____ 2. BAILEY   B. Wouldn't treat Marguerite's tooth
_____ 3. MARY   C. World champion Black boxer
_____ 4. WEALTH   D. Enviable attribute of whites
_____ 5. VIVIAN BAXTER   E. Marguerite was first Negro to work there
_____ 6. REV. THOMAS   F. Marguerite drove home from this place
_____ 7. DR. LINCOLN   G. Marguerite's new name
_____ 8. LOUISE KENDRICKS   H. Had false teeth knocked out
_____ 9. TRAIN   I. Children's mother
_____ 10. ST. LOUIS   J. Owner of Store in Stamps
_____ 11. JOE LOUIS   K. Author of autobiography
_____ 12. SAN FRANCISCO   L. Johnson children's method of travel to Stamps
_____ 13. POWHITETRASH   M. Bailey's first love
_____ 14. UNCLE WILLIE   N. Daddy Bailey's home
_____ 15. LOS ANGELES   O. Marguerite's brother
_____ 16. JOYCE   P. Marguerite's home in high school
_____ 17. MEXICO   Q. Daddy Bailey took children there
_____ 18. STREET CARS   R. Marguerite's girlfriend
_____ 19. MOMMA   S. Mocked and insulted Momma
_____ 20. SEGREGATION   T. Complete in Stamps

MATCHING WORKSHEET 2 - *I Know Why The Caged Bird Sings*

_____ 1. BAILEY   A. What Louise taught Marguerite to do
_____ 2. STREET CARS   B. Gave Marguerite the gift of books
_____ 3. MRS. CULLINAN   C. Marguerite was the first Negro to work there
_____ 4. DOLORES   D. City in Arkansas where author lived
_____ 5. MRS. FLOWERS   E. Fought with Marguerite and cut her
_____ 6. MR. FREEMAN   F. Changed Marguerite's name to Mary
_____ 7. GIGGLE   G. "Mother Dear"
_____ 8. GRANDMOTHER   H. Result of Marguerite's seduction
_____ 9. HENDERSON   I. Marguerite's first white love
_____ 10. JUNK YARD   J. Got carried away at church services
_____ 11. KLAN   K. Owner of the Store
_____ 12. LOYAL   L. Author of autobiography
_____ 13. MAYA ANGELOU   M. Sexually abused Marguerite
_____ 14. MOMMA   N. Momma's last name
_____ 15. SISTER MONROE   O. This Baxter was precinct captain in St. Louis
_____ 16. PREGNANT   P. Attribute of Baxter clan
_____ 17. SHAKESPEARE   Q. Marguerite's brother
_____ 18. STAMPS   R. Saw his dead wife in a dream
_____ 19. MR. TAYLOR   S. Searching for a Black man
_____ 20. VIVIAN BAXTER   T. Marguerite lived here for one month

ANSWER KEYS: MATCHING WORKSHEETS - *Caged Bird*

	#1	#2
1.	K	Q
2.	O	C
3.	G	F
4.	D	E
5.	I	B
6.	H	M
7.	B	A
8.	R	O
9.	L	N
10.	Q	T
11.	C	S
12.	P	P
13.	S	L
14.	A	K
15.	N	J
16.	M	H
17.	F	I
18.	E	D
19.	J	R
20.	T	G

JUGGLE LETTER REVIEW GAME - *I Know Why The Caged Bird Sings*

SCRAMBLED	WORD	CLUE
LYEIBA	BAILEY	Marguerite's brother
ALINLNUC	CULLINAN	Mrs. ___ changed Marguerite's name
REOLOSD	DOLORES	Cut Marguerite in a fight
SEWROFL	FLOWERS	Mrs. ___ gave Marguerite the gift of books
NEAREFM	FREEMAN	Mr. ___ sexually abused Marguerite
GLGEGI	GIGGLE	What Louise taught Marguerite to do
NEMHRRGDTAO	GRANDMOTHER	This Baxter was precinct captain in St. Louis
EDRONHNES	HENDERSON	Momma's last name
OJUSEILO	JOE LOUIS	World champion Black boxer
CEJYO	JOYCE	Bailey's first love
DKRYAJNU	JUNK YARD	Marguerite lived here for one month
NAKL	KLAN	Searching for a Black man
OCLNNLI	LINCOLN	Dr. ___ wouldn't treat Marguerite's tooth
SEGASLNELO	LOS ANGELES	Daddy Bailey's home
UIOSEL	LOUISE	Marguerite's first friend
OALLY	LOYAL	Attribute of Baxter clan
ARMY	MARY	Marguerite's new name
OYGMLUAAENA	MAYA ANGELOU	Author of autobiography
EXCMOI	MEXICO	Marguerite drove home from this place
AMOMM	MOMMA	Owner of Store
NEROMO	MONROE	Sister ___ got carried away at church services
EPHTHOIRSTAW	POWHITETRASH	Mocked and insulted Momma
EPTNNGAR	PREGNANT	Result of Marguerite's seduction
NSNCOAIFSRAC	SAN FRANCISCO	Marguerite's home in high school
REOENIGGTAS	SEGREGATION	Complete in Stamps
SRESEKHPEAA	SHAKESPEARE	Marguerite's first white love
PASSMT	STAMPS	City in Arkansas where author lived
ILOUSST	ST. LOUIS	Daddy Bailey took children there
RTRTCSAEE	STREET CARS	Marguerite was first Negro to work there
YTLARO	TAYLOR	Mr. ___ saw his dead wife in a dream
OSATHM	THOMAS	Rev. ___ had false teeth knocked out
AIRNT	TRAIN	Johnson children's method of travel to Stamps

VOCABULARY RESOURCE MATERIALS

I Know Why The Caged Bird Sings Vocabulary Word Search

```
E  J  A  U  N  T  I  N  E  S  S  A  M  A  L  A  I  S  E
S  S  K  P  Q  E  N  I  G  M  A  T  C  F  Y  P  R  T  M
T  M  A  R  A  U  D  I  N  G  J  E  O  D  R  R  K  L  B
H  S  U  O  R  E  N  O  I  Q  J  F  H  W  G  M  N  N  E
E  K  A  X  K  P  B  S  T  W  S  F  E  M  O  Y  Q  X  Z
T  S  I  I  S  B  Z  S  T  R  X  A  R  T  G  S  Q  D  Z
I  C  O  M  M  E  N  S  U  R  A  T  E  H  C  U  A  G  L
C  H  N  I  S  V  Y  O  B  P  S  B  N  M  A  O  M  Q  E
S  C  A  T  S  L  D  C  E  P  E  J  T  N  R  N  C  C  E
P  M  R  Y  O  A  M  T  R  T  G  R  D  Q  T  I  U  A  L
A  B  A  Q  B  O  A  N  E  L  B  A  C  S  D  M  P  J  B
R  B  P  U  R  P  P  B  Z  D  R  W  E  I  E  O  L  O  A
S  S  O  O  I  D  A  D  I  Y  I  R  P  N  L  X  O  L  T
E  R  S  S  Q  R  W  Y  C  C  U  O  I  F  E  I  Y  E  U
T  E  S  X  U  O  V  F  A  T  Y  C  U  U  M  H  O  D  R
C  I  J  D  E  L  Y  B  R  C  A  N  G  S  M  K  Q  U  C
D  W  P  J  T  L  T  E  T  L  Q  A  I  E  A  W  Y  T  S
F  L  O  R  I  D  P  Y  S  T  M  R  M  C  R  B  P  D  N
L  A  C  E  R  A  T  I  O  N  E  S  N  E  T  E  R  P  I
```

ABET	ENIGMA	MOROSE	RANCOR
APERTURES	ESTHETIC	MOTE	REBUTTING
CAJOLED	FLORID	OMINOUS	SOBRIQUET
COHERENT	GAUCHE	ONEROUS	SPARSE
COMMENSURATE	INFUSE	OSTRACIZE	SUPERCILIOUS
CYNIC	INSCRUTABLE	PARANOIA	TAFFETA
DISSIPATE	JAUNTINESS	PLOY	TEDIOUS
DROLL	LACERATION	PRETENSE	TRAMMELED
ECUMENICAL	MALAISE	PROXIMITY	TROUBADOURS
EMBEZZLE	MARAUDING	QUANDARY	

I Know Why The Caged Bird Sings Vocabulary Word Search Answer Key

```
E J A U N T I N E S S A M A L A I S E
S     P     E N I G M A T C           M
T M A R A U D I N G     O             B
H S U O R E N O I T     H     M       E
E   A   X         T   S F A     O     Z
T   I   I         S T R A R T   S Q   Z
I   C O M M E N S U R A T E H C U A G L
C   N   I         O B P   N A O N   E
S   A   T   S D   E   E   T N   I   C
P   R   Y O A M T R   R   D     M   A
A   A   O B O A E     A C S D   P J B
R   P   P     B Z D   C E I E   O O A
S   O   O I D A   I Y I R   N L O L T
S   R   S Q R     C C U O I F E I Y U
E   S   S U O     A T Y C U M   O D R
T   E   S U O     R   A N S M   O U C
    I       E L     T L   A I E A   S
D           T L         S   R C R   N
F L O   R I D P     S       R   R   I
L A C E R A T I O N E S N E T E R P I
```

ABET	ENIGMA	MOROSE	RANCOR
APERTURES	ESTHETIC	MOTE	REBUTTING
CAJOLED	FLORID	OMINOUS	SOBRIQUET
COHERENT	GAUCHE	ONEROUS	SPARSE
COMMENSURATE	INFUSE	OSTRACIZE	SUPERCILIOUS
CYNIC	INSCRUTABLE	PARANOIA	TAFFETA
DISSIPATE	JAUNTINESS	PLOY	TEDIOUS
DROLL	LACERATION	PRETENSE	TRAMMELED
ECUMENICAL	MALAISE	PROXIMITY	TROUBADOURS
EMBEZZLE	MARAUDING	QUANDARY	

I Know Why The Caged Bird Sings Vocabulary Crossword

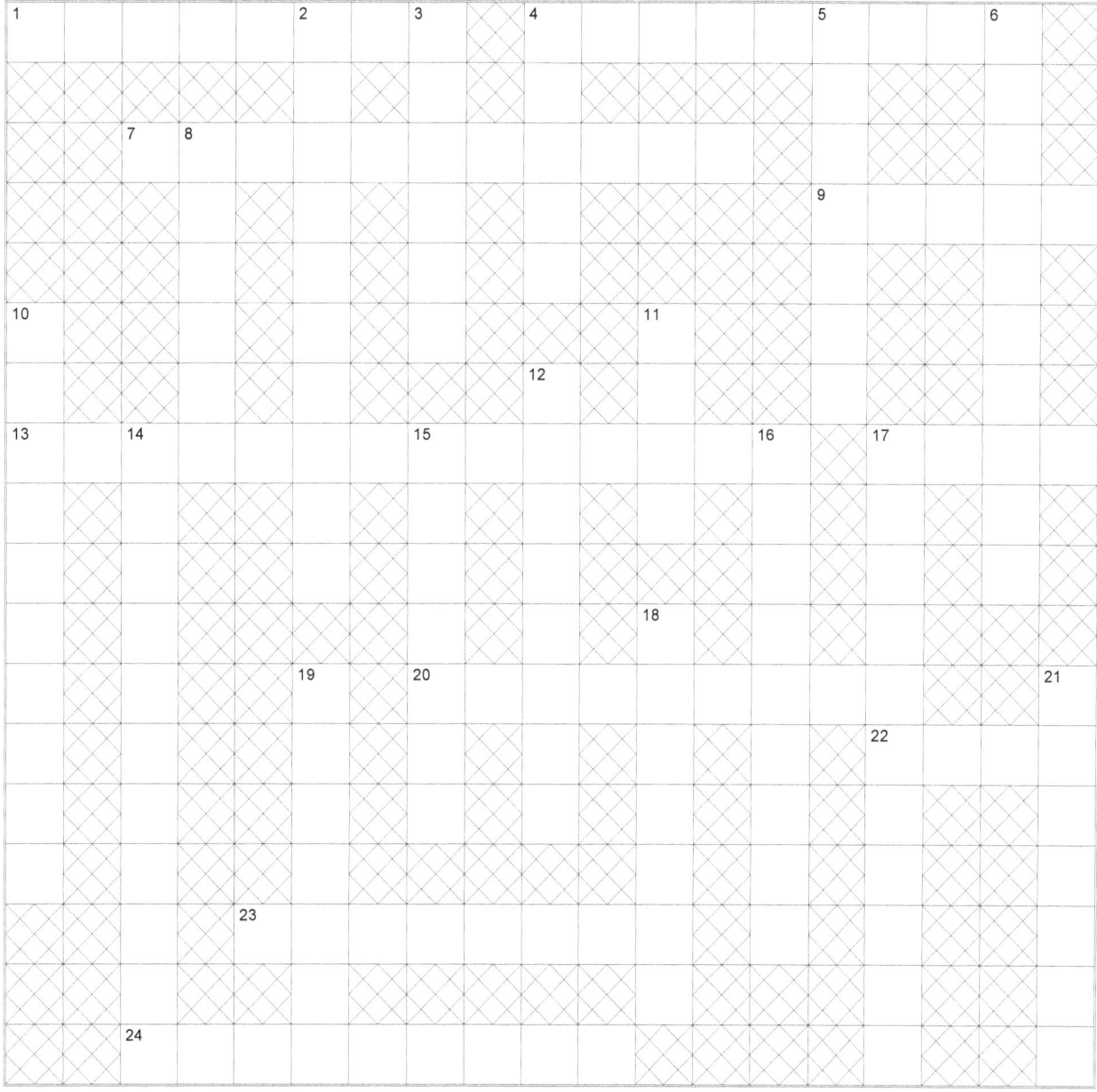

Across
1. quickness; skillfulness
4. Mentally skillful
7. Strolling minstrels
9. One who believes others are selfish
13. Impulsiveness
17. An action done to frustrate
20. To exclude from a group
22. A speck
23. Sticking together
24. To drive away; disperse

Down
2. Promoting unity among religions
3. Occurring at widely spaced intervals
4. Amusingly odd
5. Rough-sounding
6. Expressing care or concern
8. Bitter, long-lasting resentment
10. A jagged, deep cut
11. To encourage or help
12. Appreciating beauty
14. committed
15. Troublesome
16. An affectionate nickname
17. Wild uproar or noise
18. A crisp fabric with a slight sheen
19. Menacing; threatening
21. Tiresome due to extreme slowness

I Know Why The Caged Bird Sings Vocabulary Crossword Answer Key

Across
1. quickness; skillfulness
4. Mentally skillful
7. Strolling minstrels
9. One who believes others are selfish
13. Impulsiveness
17. An action done to frustrate
20. To exclude from a group
22. A speck
23. Sticking together
24. To drive away; disperse

Down
2. Promoting unity among religions
3. Occurring at widely spaced intervals
4. Amusingly odd
5. Rough-sounding
6. Expressing care or concern
8. Bitter, long-lasting resentment
10. A jagged, deep cut
11. To encourage or help
12. Appreciating beauty
14. committed
15. Troublesome
16. An affectionate nickname
17. Wild uproar or noise
18. A crisp fabric with a slight sheen
19. Menacing; threatening
21. Tiresome due to extreme slowness

VOCABULARY WORKSHEET 1 *I Know Why the Caged Bird Sings*

Directions: Place the letter of the matching definition on the blank line.

____ 1.	dexterous	A.	skillful
____ 2.	supercilious	B.	calmed; soothed
____ 3.	perpetrated	C.	those who get pleasure from being mistreated
____ 4.	recriminations	D.	expressing care or concern
____ 5.	provincials	E.	committed
____ 6.	retributive	F.	revealing no emotion
____ 7.	elocution	G.	troublesome
____ 8.	mollified	H.	having a buoyant or self-confident air
____ 9.	ecumenical	I.	promoting unity among religions
____ 10.	impassivity	J.	showing haughty disdain
____ 11.	nonchalance	K.	cool indifference
____ 12.	appellations	L.	countercharges
____ 13.	cynic	M.	acting in a patronizingly superior way
____ 14.	debutante	N.	demanded in repayment
____ 15.	jauntiness	O.	a young woman formally entering society
____ 16.	masochists	P.	unsophisticated people
____ 17.	condescension	Q.	sticking together
____ 18.	coherent	R.	names, titles, or designations
____ 19.	onerous	S.	public speaking
____ 20.	solicitous	T.	one who believes others are selfish

ANSWER KEY VOCABULARY WORKSHEET 1 *I Know Why the Caged Bird Sings*

A.	1.	dexterous	A.	skillful	
J.	2.	supercilious	B.	calmed; soothed	
E.	3.	perpetrated	C.	those who get pleasure from being mistreated	
L.	4.	recriminations	D.	expressing care or concern	
P.	5.	provincials	E.	committed	
N.	6.	retributive	F.	revealing no emotion	
S.	7.	elocution	G.	troublesome	
B.	8.	mollified	H.	having a buoyant or self-confident air	
I.	9.	ecumenical	I.	promoting unity among religions	
F.	10.	impassivity	J.	showing haughty disdain	
K.	11.	nonchalance	K.	cool indifference	
R.	12.	appellation	L.	countercharges	
T.	13.	cynic	M.	acting in a patronizingly superior way	
O.	14.	debutante	N.	demanded in repayment	
H.	15.	jauntiness	O.	a young woman formally entering society	
C.	16.	masochists	P.	unsophisticated people	
M.	17.	condescension	Q.	sticking together	
Q.	18.	coherent	R.	names, titles, or designations	
G.	19.	onerous	S.	public speaking	
D.	20.	solicitous	T.	one who believes others are selfish	

VOCABULARY WORKSHEET 2 *I Know Why the Caged Bird Sings*

_____ 1. wandering minstrels
   A. appellations   B. tribulations   C. masochists   D. troubadours

_____ 2. extreme, irrational distrust of others
   A. paranoia   B. jauntiness   C. impertinence   D. pretense

_____ 3. out of proper or chronological order
   A. perpetrated   B. anachronism   C. deferential   D. esthetic

_____ 4. menacing, threatening
   A. malaise   B. capriciousness   C. ostensibly   D. ominous

_____ 5. an affectionate nickname
   A. cynic   B. sobriquet   C. ploy   D. taffeta

_____ 6. revealing no emotion
   A. impassivity   B. rancor   C. quandary   D. expeditious

_____ 7. gloomy
   A. blasphemous   B. florid   C. inscrutable   D. morose

_____ 8. a speck
   A. mote   B. sparse   C. infuse   D. taffeta

_____ 9. of the same size or proportion
   A. nonchalance   B. droll   C. commensurate   D. expeditious

_____ 10. rough-sounding
   A. cacophony   B. raucous   C. pandemonium   D. blasphemous

_____ 11. dried out, arid
   A. inscrutable   B. retributive   C. desiccated   D. onerous

_____ 12. refuting
   A. rebutting   B. ostracized   C. dexterous   D. admonished

_____ 13. intensely painful
   A. morose   B. sparse   C. inscrutable   D. excruciating

_____ 14. something puzzling or inexplicable
   A. expeditious   B. enigma   C. solicitous   D. florid

_____ 15. raiding to plunder
   A. impertinence   B. perpetrated   C. marauding   D. capriciousness

_____ 16. middle class
   A. bourgeoisie   B. apertures   C. aphorisms   D. pandemonium

_____ 17. pertaining to the devil
   A. quandary   B. sparse   C. deftness   D. diabolic

_____ 18. tiresome due to extreme slowness
   A. droll   B. tedious   C. inscrutable   D. expeditious

_____ 19. a jagged, deep cut
   A. frivolity   B. elocution   C. laceration   D. cacophony

_____ 20. to take money or property in violation of a trust
   A. coherent   B. expeditious   C. embezzle   D. condescension

VOCABULARY WORKSHEET 2 *I Know Why the Caged Bird Sings*

1. wandering minstrels
   A. appellations   B. tribulations   C. masochists   D. **troubadours**
2. extreme, irrational distrust of others
   A. **paranoia**   B. jauntiness   C. impertinence   D. pretense
3. out of proper or chronological order
   A. perpetrated   B. **anachronism**   C. deferential   D. esthetic
4. menacing, threatening
   A. malaise   B. capriciousness   C. ostensibly   D. **ominous**
5. an affectionate nickname
   A. cynic   B. **sobriquet**   C. ploy   D. taffeta
6. revealing no emotion
   A. **impassivity**   B. rancor   C. quandary   D. expeditious
7. gloomy
   A. blasphemous   B. florid   C. inscrutable   D. **morose**
8. a speck
   A. **mote**   B. sparse   C. infuse   D. taffeta
9. of the same size or proportion
   A. nonchalance   B. droll   C. **commensurate**   D. expeditious
10. rough-sounding
    A. cacophony   B. **raucous**   C. pandemonium   D. blasphemous
11. dried out, arid
    A. inscrutable   B. retributive   C. **desiccated**   D. onerous
12. refuting
    A. **rebutting**   B. ostracized   C. dexterous   D. admonished
13. intensely painful
    A. morose   B. sparse   C. inscrutable   D. **excruciating**
14. something puzzling or inexplicable
    A. expeditious   B. **enigma**   C. solicitous   D. florid
15. raiding to plunder
    A. impertinence   B. perpetrated   C. **marauding**   D. capriciousness
16. middle class
    A. **bourgeoisie**   B. apertures   C. aphorisms   D. pandemonium
17. pertaining to the devil
    A. quandary   B. sparse   C. deftness   D. **diabolic**
18. tiresome due to extreme slowness
    A. droll   B. **tedious**   C. inscrutable   D. expeditious
19. a jagged, deep cut
    A. frivolity   B. elocution   C. **laceration**   D. cacophony
20. to take money or property in violation of a trust
    A. coherent   B. expeditious   C. **embezzle**   D. condescension

VOCABULARY JUGGLE LETTER REVIEW GAME *I Know Why the Caged Bird Sings*

SCRAMBLED	WORD	CLUE
EATB	ABET	to encourage or help
AONRNHCSMAI	ANACHRONISM	out of proper or chronological order
DONSIMEADH	ADMONISHED	gently reproved
SEATURRPE	APERTURES	openings
SPLOIEATNAPL	APPELLATIONS	names, titles, or designations
POANORAPBTI	APPROBATION	an expression of warm approval; praise
IRMASPSHO	APHORISMS	brief statements of principles
SESMAELOBPU	BLASPHEMOUS	speaking irreverently of a sacred entity
RGEOBUISOEI	BOURGEOISIE	the middle class
PNCOHYAOC	CACOPHONY	jarring, discordant sound
LCOJEDA	CAJOLED	urged gently
IIEOUNRCSACPSS	CAPRICIOUSNESS	impulsiveness
HRNCTOEE	COHERENT	sticking together
AEOMEUMNTRCS	COMMENSURATE	of the same size or proportion
NCOISECNNOSED	CONDESCENSION	acting in a patronizingly superior way
YCCNI	CYNIC	one who believes others are selfish
ETUNADBET	DEBUTANTE	a young woman entering society
TENILEFREDA	DEFERENTIAL	courteous, respectful
SNEDETSF	DEFTNESS	quickness ; skillfulness
ETCCSADIDE	DESICCATED	dried out, arid
XTUEOESDR	DEXTEROUS	mentally skillful
COLAABLIID	DIABOLICAL	characteristic of the devil
TISIAEDSP	DISSIPATE	to drive away; disperse
OLRLD	DROLL	amusingly odd
AGNIEM	ENIGMA	something puzzling or inexplicable
TICEAUNEN	ENUNCIATE	to pronounce; articulate
CNLCAEUEMI	ECUMENICAL	promoting unity among religions
COTUNIOEL	ELOCUTION	public speaking
ZBMZEEEL	EMBEZZLE	to take money or property and violate a trust
HICTTSEE	ESTHETIC	appreciating beauty
NCECIURTGXAI	EXCRUCIATING	intensely painful
TEDIOXSUEPI	EXPEDITIOUS	done with speed and efficiency
YFMBALAOTN	FLAMBOYANT	highly elaborate, showy
ROLFDI	FLORID	rosy colored
LVSOUOFIR	FRIVOLOUS	silly

UEAHGC	GAUCHE	lacking social polish; tactless
RPITCENEIMNE	IMPERTINENCE	boldness
AVTYSSIMIIP	IMPASSIVITY	revealing no emotion
FSNIEU	INFUSE	to fill with something
RINTULSECAB	INSCRUTABLE	difficult to understand
USATJSENNI	JAUNTINESS	having a buoyant or self-confident air
ENTACRALIO	LACERATION	a jagged, deep cut
IDGRAUMAN	MARAUDING	raiding to plunder
IAMALES	MALAISE	a general sense of depression
SOSSTHACMI	MASOCHISTS	those who get pleasure from being mistreated
EOSOMR	MOROSE	gloomy
IFLOEIDLM	MOLLIFIED	calmed, soothed
TOEM	MOTE	a speck
EHLAACNONNC	NONCHALANCE	coolly unconcerned or indifferent
MOUINSO	OMINOUS	menacing; threatening
NOUOSRE	ONEROUS	troublesome
ENYSOSLIBT	OSTENSIBLY	appearing as such
ETCAIROSZ	OSTRACIZE	to exclude from a group.
LLBAAPEP	PALPABLE	capable of being touched or felt
DMNEOINPUMA	PANDEMONIUM	wild uproar or noise
RNAAIAPO	PARANOIA	extreme, irrational distrust of other
RPTTAPEEEDR	PERPETRATED	committed
YOPL	PLOY	an action done to frustrate
RSNPEEET	PRETENSE	false appearance
RACIVSONLIP	PROVINCIALS	unsophisticated people
RMTYOPXII	PROXIMITY	closeness
NQADYRAU	QUANDARY	a state of uncertainty or perplexity
RRONAC	RANCOR	bitter, long-lasting resentment
SUOUARC	RAUCOUS	rough-sounding
TBITRNEGU	REBUTTING	refuting
IORANRNTMCSIIE	RECRIMINATIONS	countercharges
IBITERTVRUE	RETRIBUTIVE	demanded in repayment
QITSOBRUE	SOBRIQUET	an affectionate nickname
ITCSILUSOO	SOLICITOUS	expressing care or concern.
PSESAR	SPARSE	occurring at widely spaced intervals
OUSSEUICILRP	SUPERCILIOUS	showing haughty disdain
TFEATAF	TAFFETA	a crisp fabric with a slight sheen

DIOETSU	TEDIOUS	tiresome due to extreme slowness
LTEMREDMA	TRAMMELED	restricted, restrained
SITOTIBLRANU	TRIBULATIONS	suffering
SDOUUOTBARR	TROUBADOURS	strolling minstrels